REGENTS CONTINENTAL DRAMA SERIES

General Editor: John Loftis

THE KNIGHT OF OLMEDO

LOPE DE VEGA

The Knight of Olmedo

(El caballero de Olmedo)

The Spanish Text with a Facing English Translation

Translated and Edited by
WILLARD F. KING

UNIVERSITY OF NEBRASKA PRESS · LINCOLN

MANUFACTURED IN THE UNITED STATES OF AMERICA

CONTENTS

REGENTS CONTINENTAL DRAMA SERIES

The Regents Continental Drama Series will provide editions of a group of plays chosen from the periods of highest achievement in the national dramas of Western Europe. Intended to make the plays more readily accessible to English and American students, the editions will include on facing pages the text in the original language and a translation: ordinarily a prose translation, as literal as is consistent with idiomatic English. The introduction will supply information on the date of the play, its place in the author's career, its stage history, its textual history, its sources, as well as a critical interpretation. Explanatory notes are directed to the needs of mature students who are not specialists in the Continental literatures. Textual notes are provided only in instances of unusual interest. Spelling and punctuation are modernized along consciously conservative lines.

The editor and publisher have planned the series with attention to the international quality of European drama, the shared patterns of development evident in plays produced in different countries and in different centuries. It is their hope that the series will aid in the comparative study of European drama—too often frustrated because only a few men can have the linguistic skills required to read several languages without the assistance of translations.

JOHN LOFTIS

Stanford University

LIST OF ABBREVIATIONS

1641   *Veinticuatro parte perfecta de las comedias del Fénix de España, Frey Lope Félix de Vega Carpio* . . . Zaragoza: Pedro Vergés, 1641.

B   *El caballero de Olmedo*, ed. José Manuel Blecua. 3rd ed. Zaragoza: Ebro, 1947.

C   Covarrubias, Sebastián. *Tesoro de la lengua castellana o española (1611)*, ed. Martín de Riquer. Barcelona: Horta, 1943.

DA   *Diccionario de la lengua castellana.* 5 vols. Madrid: Real Academia Española, 1726-1737. [Commonly known as *Diccionario de autoridades.*]

H   *Comedias escogidas de Frey Lope Félix de Vega Carpio*, ed. Juan Eugenio Hartzenbusch, in Biblioteca de Autores Españoles, Vol. 34. Madrid: Rivadeneyra, 1855.

J   *Obras dramáticas escogidas* [de Lope], ed. Eduardo Juliá Martínez, in Biblioteca Clásica, Vol. 268. Madrid: Librería y Casa Editorial Hernando, 1935.

M   *El caballero de Olmedo*, ed. I. I. Macdonald. Cambridge: Cambridge University Press, 1934.

R   *El caballero de Olmedo*, ed. Francisco Rico. Madrid: Anaya, 1967.

RAE   *Obras de Lope de Vega*, Vol. X, ed. Marcelino Menéndez y Pelayo. Madrid: Real Academia Española, 1899.

S.D.   stage direction

INTRODUCTION

El caballero de Olmedo was first published in Zaragoza in 1641 in *Parte XXIV* of the plays of Lope de Vega.[1] The play was written, however, long before its publication, although the exact date of composition is not ascertainable. On the basis of their study of changes over the years in Lope's practices with regard to dramatic versification, Morley and Bruerton assign the play to the years between 1615 and 1626, most probably 1620-1625.[2] Perhaps the time spread can be narrowed to 1618-1621, for the title of the play does not appear in the list of 333 dramas Lope claimed to have written which he attached to the sixth edition of his *Peregrino en su patria*, published in 1618. Further, the ballad beginning "Por la tarde salió Inés" (vs. 75) appears, with insignificant variants, in an anthology of poems gathered together by Pedro Arias Pérez under the title of *Primavera y flor de los mejores romances* and published in Madrid in 1621. To be sure, the ballad could have been composed before the play and later inserted in *El caballero* as Alonso's initial eulogy of Inés (Lope not infrequently made a sonnet or a ballad serve multiple purposes); but in this case, as Francisco Rico observes in his edition of the play,[3] the reference to the "feria de Medina" present in both versions of the ballad would lead to the assumption that the anthologist was copying from the play and not vice versa: the Medina fair is a natural place for Inés to be seen within the context of the play but without point or relevance in the isolated ballad.

El caballero de Olmedo is then the work of the mature Lope (born in 1562, he was fifty-three in 1615, the earliest date suggested for the composition of the play), confident master of every dramatic technique, in full control of his means of expression—and dealing with his favorite theme of love. Twice married, the ardent lover of several mistresses (even after he

---

1. A *parte* (volume) usually contained twelve plays.
2. S. Griswold Morley and Courtney Bruerton, *The Chronology of Lope de Vega's "Comedias"* (New York: MLA, 1940), pp. 177-178.
3. (Madrid: Anaya, 1967), p. 43, and p. 72, note 14.

became a priest in 1614), Lope never wrote a play in which love plays no part; but *El caballero* is perhaps his supreme tribute to the radiant charm of new young love.[4]

As in the case of a number of the better-known plays in Lope's enormous repertory, such as *Peribáñez* or *Fuenteovejuna*, no records of seventeenth-century performances of *El caballero* have yet been discovered. General familiarity with Lope's drama and the legends surrounding the Knight of Olmedo is suggested, however, by the existence of an excellent dramatic parody—based in part on Lope's tragedy—of the knight's life and love; also entitled *El caballero de Olmedo*, it was written by Francisco Antonio de Monteser and played before King Philip IV himself in 1651. We know that in the eighteenth century Lope's play was performed in Valencia;[5] and in the years 1933 to 1935 Federico García Lorca's travelling theatrical troupe of university students known as La Barraca played his adaptation of *El caballero* (which the poet once praised as among the most important works in the history of world theater) with great success all over Spain.[6] In 1935, on the occasion of the third centenary of Lope's death, the drama was performed in Cambridge, England. In 1961, Jill Booty published English prose translations of five of Lope's plays, including the *Caballero*.[7] The latest French translation, also in prose, was made by Albert Camus and performed with considerable critical and popular success in June, 1957, during the drama festival at Angers. Camus closes the brief prologue to his translation with a heartfelt tribute to Lope's theater: "In a Europe reduced to ashes, Lope de Vega and the Spanish theater [of the

---

4. The fullest and most reliable account of the life of Lope de Vega is still to be found in Américo Castro and Hugo A. Rennert, *Vida de Lope de Vega*, 2nd ed. (Madrid: Anaya, 1968).

5. Monteser's burlesque play is printed in *Biblioteca de Autores Españoles* 49 (Madrid: Rivadeneyra, 1859): 157-171; for a discussion of it and the dating of its performance in 1651, see A. Restori, review of M. Pelayo, *Obras de Lope de Vega*, X, in *Zeitschrift für Romanische Philologie* 29 (1905): 358-365. For the Valencia performance of Lope's drama, see E[duardo] Juliá [Martínez], "Preferencias teatrales del público valenciano en el siglo XVIII," *Revista de Filología Española* 20(1933): 113-159.

6. García Lorca's adaptation of the drama eliminates the final three scenes of the play, after the death of Alonso, which he believed had been added by Lope in deference to the contemporary taste for bloody vengeance. For a discussion of the composition, activities, and repertoire of La Barraca, Lorca's own account is of great interest (see his *Obras completas*, 14th ed. [Madrid: Aguilar, 1968], pp. 1747-1789; his remarks about *El caballero* are found on p. 1786).

7. Lope de Vega, *Five Plays*, intr. R. D. F. Pring-Mill (New York: Hill and Wang, 1961).

Golden Age] can contribute to us today their inexhaustible radiance, their extraordinary youthfulness, can help us to find once again on our stage the spirit of grandeur ultimately required for the true future of our theater."[8]

The present edition of *El caballero de Olmedo* is based on the only known seventeenth-century text of the play, which appears on fols. 43^r through 62^v (misnumbered 61^v) of *Parte XXIV* of Lope's plays, published, as indicated earlier, in Zaragoza in 1641, six years after the author's death. No autograph manuscript of *El caballero* exists, and nothing guarantees that the 1641 printed text is a faithful copy of Lope's original. Lope did not write his plays for publication; frequently he did not keep a copy of a play he had sold to a company of actors. Even during Lope's lifetime the printed versions may be poor texts based, perhaps, on an actor's defective copy of the play; and even when Lope claimed to have supervised the publication of a *parte*, he does not allege that the texts are perfect, either because he no longer possessed his original manuscript or because he had little time to make the necessary corrections. Lope announces in the dedication to his *Parte IX*, for example, that all the plays contained therein reproduce his original manuscripts, but the text of *La dama boba* printed in it is 413 lines shorter than that of the autograph manuscript of this play, which has, fortunately, come down to us also.[9]

Thus, the text of *El caballero* printed in *Parte XXIV*, published posthumously, inspires little confidence. There are a number of typographical errors (silently corrected in the text printed here), two lacunae of undeterminable length revealed by a break in the pattern of versification (following vss. 1017 and 2709), and a number of difficult, possibly garbled, lines of obscure meaning and syntax which receive comment in the notes. The play is, if not exceptional for its brevity within the norms of Lope's practice, still short, and the reader or spectator is entitled to wonder if a few scenes are not missing. Certainly the transition between Alonso's opening soliloquy and the following conversation between the previously unidentified Fabia and Tello is discon-

---

8. "Dans notre Europe de cendres, Lope de Vega et le théâtre espagnol peuvent apporter aujourd'hui leur inépuisable lumière, leur insolite jeunesse, nous aider à retrouver sur nos scènes l'esprit de grandeur pour servir enfin l'avenir véritable de notre théâtre" (*Le Chevalier d'Olmedo* [Paris: Gallimard, 1957], p. 11).

9. See Castro and Rennert, op. cit., pp. 239-352, and Morley and Bruerton, op. cit., pp. 7-11, for discussion of the transmission of Lope's texts.

certingly abrupt, and later on (see notes 40 and 44) there are puzzling casual references to incidents the audience seems to be expected to know about but which have not been acted out before it. Nevertheless, in view of the absence of other seventeenth-century texts, this edition reproduces that of 1641 with considerable faithfulness, departing from it only in a conservative modernization of punctuation (no asides are indicated in 1641, nor have they been added in this Spanish text); in the deletion of the cast of characters printed at the beginning of each act; in the expansion of the contracted forms of character names in speech prefixes; and in the marking by indentation of the beginning of each new stanza. In general, except for accentuation, spelling has not been modernized; Lope's differs so little from modern spelling that no reader should be confused by it, and modernization would at times spoil the rhyme scheme (e.g., see textual note to vs. 1719).

The 1641 text has been collated with the principal modern editions of the play, and the first occurrence of important variant readings is indicated in the textual notes. The first modern editor, Juan Eugenio Hartzenbusch, in his edition of *El caballero* in 1855, resolved almost all of the difficulties of the 1641 text intelligently; his emendations have been adopted very nearly *in toto* by later editors, and frequently without acknowledgment. A comparison of the Spanish text and the English translation here given will show at a glance what stage directions have been added in English to the sparse indications provided in the original, which, as was Lope's custom, skillfully sets the scene and signals the time within the dramatic dialogue itself.

In the sense that several of the leading characters of *El caballero* really lived and their deeds are recorded on the pages of Spanish chronicles, the play is a historical drama. It is evident, however, that Lope's prime intention was not in this case, as in some measure it was in a play like *Fuenteovejuna*, to recreate a historical conflict, and the sources upon which he drew in composing *El caballero* are complicated, varied, and treated with the maximum of imaginative freedom. It should likewise be remembered that some of these sources were immediately obvious to the contemporary Spanish audience as they could not have been to an English audience of the same time. First and foremost, he had a popular *seguidilla*, a little refrain known to everybody for a century or so, namely, the ominous warning lines sung by the Peasant near the end of the last act:

> Que de noche le mataron
> al caballero,
> la gala de Medina,
> la flor de Olmedo.

> (So by night they killed him,
> the noble knight,
> glory of Medina,
> flower of Olmedo.)

These lines alone provided him with his hero, a "verray, parfit gentil knight," the scene of the action, and the denouement, the dark, mysterious murder of the protagonist.

In 1622 Alonso López de Haro in his *Nobiliario genealógico de los reyes de España* informed his readers that the little song commemorated the murder of Don Juan de Vivero, Knight of Santiago, husband of Beatriz de Guzmán, by one Miguel Ruiz, who had attacked Don Juan for reasons of personal differences as the latter was returning to Olmedo from Medina after a bullfight. Depending upon the date of composition of his drama, it may have been possible for Lope to read Haro's account of the murder in manuscript or printed form. It is possible also that he was aware of oral traditions from Medina del Campo about the Knight of Olmedo and that, in fact, he knew, as we now do, that Juan de Vivero was killed in 1521 during the reign of Charles V;[10] but if

---

10. Miguel Ruiz, accompanied by several others, attacked and killed Juan de Vivero with a lance on Nov. 6, 1521, but the motive of the assault remains obscure. Some accounts suggest a quarrel over greyhounds, others suggest political revenge; but no one attributes the murder to the jealousy of a scorned suitor. Whether or not Lope knew the real name of the Knight of Olmedo (i.e., Juan de Vivero), when he called his hero and heroine Alonso and Inés, by accident or design he gave them the real names of the historical knight's great-grandparents: *Inés* de Guzmán and *Alonso* Pérez de Vivero, a high official in the court of Juan II, friend of the Lord High Constable Alvaro de Luna, and the victim of a treacherous murder in 1452. For the quotation in Spanish from López de Haro as well as extracts from almost all the pertinent documents having to do with Juan de Vivero, see Fidel Fita, "El Memorial histórico de Medina del Campo," "El caballero de Olmedo y la Orden de Santiago," "Don Rodrigo de Vivero y Velasco . . .," *Boletín de la Real Academia de la Historia* 46 (1905): 325-349, 398-422, 452-474; Francisco Rico, introduction to his edition of *El caballero*, pp. 26-29; Joseph Pérez. "La mort du Chevalier d'Olmedo," *Mélanges à la mémoire de Jean Serrailh*, 2 (Paris: Centre de Recherches de l'Institut d'Etudes Hispaniques, 1966): 243-251; and the introduction to Pérez's edition of *El caballero* (Madrid: Castalia, 1970).

he did, then he willfully ignored the historical facts as he wrote his play. It is far more likely that he knew about the historical knight no more than what the popular song said.

The legend of the knight, as preserved in these short lines of verse, had also given rise in 1606 to the composition of an inferior play by an unknown author which likewise bears the title *El caballero de Olmedo*[11] and uses the four-line refrain at a climactic moment. Once again, Lope may or may not have been familiar with this earlier dramatization of the legend; certainly his own play owes it nothing significant in expression or incidents, and, indeed, comparison of these two dramas based on the same principal source provides an exemplary demonstration of the gulf that separates genius from mediocrity. Still, certain similarities catch the reader's attention: the time of the action is pushed even farther back into the past—the reign of Enrique III (1390-1406)—than in Lope's drama; the hero's name is Alonso, and he is murdered after a bullfight by a jealous rival in love and knightly skill; and the number of his assailants is six (see vs. 2670 of Lope's Spanish text).

Without a doubt, however, Lope must have known the *Baile del caballero de Olmedo*, which exists in two versions, one anonymous and preserved in a manuscript compiled in 1615 and another (eighty-three lines in ballad form) actually published in 1617 in *Parte VII* of the plays of Lope, where it is attributed to Lope himself, though the plodding style of the composition has led almost all critics to reject the attribution vehemently. However careless Lope may have been about the published volumes of his dramas, he could not have been ignorant of the existence of the *baile*. The brief ballad recounts Alonso's love for Elvira, his brilliant performance in a bullfight and tourney at Medina, and the midnight murder on the road to Olmedo. The unpublished version possesses more interest for us because it changes the instrument of the murder from a lance to shotguns, and comments,

---

11. Ed. Eduardo Juliá Martínez in *Revista de Bibliografía Nacional*, Anejo II (Madrid: CSIC, 1944). References to a "Morales" in one manuscript of this play and to "Carrero, Telles and Salas" in the other have led some scholars to believe that the author's or authors' names are revealed in this fashion, but the arguments are not convincing.

as Lope did later (vss. 2456-2461), on the villainy of such means.[12]

If we assume that Lope knew all three of these previous literary treatments of the original popular song, they provided him only with the motive for the murder—i.e., the envy and jealousy of a scorned rival for his lady's affections, humiliated further by the hero's superior knightly prowess; none of them introduces the omens, forebodings, and mysterious apparitions—or the elaboration of the original four-line song ("Shades have warned him/ not to set out," etc.)—which loom so large in Lope's dramatization. Nor do they make any use of Lope's major literary source, Fernando de Rojas's *Tragicomedia de Calisto y Melibea* (1499), commonly called *La Celestina*, the most powerful story of tragic young lovers in all of Spanish literature.

A summary of the *Celestina* reveals how the plot and characters of this lengthy, complex "dialogued novel" are deftly reshaped to fit Lope's brief play and, ultimately, different purposes. The young nobleman Calisto chases his hawk over a garden wall and there sees and immediately falls in love with the gentle, noble Melibea. Since she rebuffs his advances severely and he burns with passion, he accepts the suggestion of his cynical, self-interested, and cowardly servant Sempronio to employ an infamous old woman called Celestina to carry his message of love to Melibea and soften her heart, despite his loyal servant Pármeno's attempt to dissuade him from this evil course. Although no rival suitors or social barriers stand in his way, neither at this time nor later does Calisto consider marriage or the necessity of protecting the honor and good name of Melibea, partly because the tenets of courtly love denied the possibility of true love within the marriage bonds, partly because he can brook no delay in the consummation of his love.

Celestina adds to the unseemly profession of go-between five other occupations—seamstress, perfume-maker, cosmetics manu-

---

12. A *baile* (dance) was a verse composition meant to be sung and danced, frequently between the acts of a play. The 1617 version is reproduced in I. I. Macdonald's edition of the *Caballero de Olmedo*, pp. 124-126; a portion of the 1615 manuscript version is reproduced and commented upon by Margit Frenk Alatorre, "Glosas de tipo popular en la antigua lírica," *Nueva Revista de Filología Hispánica* 12 (1958): 316, 320-321.

facturer, restorer of virginity, and witchcraft. She runs a sort of brothel and for money will undertake to provide the desired woman to any man; she drinks as much as she can afford to; her sanctimonious manner and dress conceal a limitless avarice and prurient interests which she can, because of her age, now satisfy only vicariously; and she is an expert witch, confident that her alliance with Satan insures the success of all her machinations. Once having gained entry into Melibea's house, by astute play on the young girl's emotions, particularly her already aroused interest in Calisto, she finally arranges a meeting by night in Melibea's garden between the two lovers and receives a gold chain from the grateful Calisto. Sempronio and Pármeno—the latter's original repugnance at dealing with Celestina having been overcome when she procures a mistress for him—kill Celestina in a fight over the golden chain; they are apprehended by the law and executed for their crime. Calisto recognizes that this noisome scandal besmirches his—not to mention Melibea's—honor but cannot bestir himself to any resolute course of action through fear of interrupting the delights of love, for the gentle Melibea has surrendered herself to him in body and in soul. However, their bliss survives only briefly the death of Celestina; strange noises outside the garden one night cause Calisto to descend the garden wall in great haste; he slips and dies immediately, his body shattered on the pavement. Unable to endure this loss, Melibea commits suicide, postponing the act only long enough to inform her unsuspecting father Pleberio of her illicit love affair. Rojas's work ends with Pleberio's lament for his adored only daughter and his outcry against the hollow illusions of happiness and the bitter, harsh deceptions of man's life in this world.

Whatever the ultimate meaning of Rojas's multifaceted work may be, there is no doubt that he intended no romantic idealization of the driving, selfish, carnal passion which led Calisto and Melibea to employ shameful means, requiring the sacrifice of family, duty, honor, to achieve brief sensual satisfaction. Love is presented as the prime example of the seductive traps the world sets for us; the lovers' flame burns briefly, consuming them and everyone they touch, leaving behind a desert waste. Yet the youth and beauty of Calisto and Melibea, the intensity of their devotion, the elegant words with which they express their passion, and the senseless cruelty of their deaths have converted them into the exemplary pair of tragic youthful lovers, the Romeo and Juliet of the Spanish world.

It is understandable why their story should have come to Lope's mind when he set out to tell his story of a knight cut down in the flower of his youth. And since the *Celestina* was almost as much a part of folk heritage as the song of the *caballero*, the audience's familiarity with it allowed him to eliminate tiresome exposition. The first sight of old Fabia with her severe dress and devout but oddly sinister manner sufficed to establish the outlines of her character and probable function in the drama without need of further explanation. The audience could be expected also to recognize with delight the echoes from the *Celestina* to be heard throughout much of the play, especially in the first encounters between Fabia and Alonso and Fabia and Inés, and appreciate Tello's motives when he asks Inés's servant whether her mistress "Melibea" is at home (vs. 1003). In the long run, though, as we shall see, the major function of the *Celestina* within the *Caballero* is to highlight the differences between Rojas's and Lope's pairs of lovers.

Perhaps, too, the fact that Calisto and Melibea belong to the fifteenth century influenced Lope's choice of chronological era for his drama. In that century the reign of Juan II of Castile (1406-1454) was remembered for its turbulence and violent conflicts but also for its gallant knights, great poets, and new elegance. What more fitting historical ambience could be found for his own knight of Olmedo, a gallant lover, poet, swordsman, violently murdered at the peak of his youthful glory? Indeed, it seems reasonable to conjecture that the action and elegiac tone of the play were partly shaped by the famous *ubi sunt* in the *Coplas* of Jorge Manrique (composed ca. 1476) inspired by the vanished glory of Juan II's reign (here cited in Longfellow's translation):

> Where is the king Don Juan? Where
> Each royal prince and noble heir
>   Of Aragon?
> Where are the courtly gallantries?
> The deeds of love and high emprise,
>   In battle done?

> Tourney and joust that charmed the eye,
> And scarf, and gorgeous panoply,
>   And nodding plume—
> What are they but a pageant scene?
> What but the garlands, gay and green,
>   That deck the tomb?
>
> Where are the high born dames, and where
> Their gay attire, and jewelled hair,
>   And odours sweet?
> Where are the gentle knights that came
> To kneel, and breathe love's ardent flame,
>   Low at their feet?
>
>   .   .   .
>
> The noble steeds, and harness bright
> And gallant lord, and stalwart knight,
>   In rich array,—
> Where shall we seek them now? Alas!
> Like the bright dewdrops on the grass,
>   They passed away.

For authentic historical incident, however, Lope consulted the chronicle-histories, probably the *Crónica de Juan II*, compiled by Lorenzo Galíndez de Carvajal (several of the specific incidents mentioned in the play—the petition to change the habit of the Order of Alcántara, Friar Vicente Ferrer's preaching, and the edicts regarding the segregation of Moors and Jews—are related consecutively in Chapters 21 and 22 of this chronicle's account of the year 1411), but historical accuracy was not his aim in *El caballero*, for events of the year 1411 are made to occur simultaneously with others that happened in 1418 or as late as 1423 (see note 61). Only the mood, atmosphere, and attitudes of the court of Juan II were important and necessary; Lope selected from the reign the minimum of real events needed to link Alonso's imagined life with the sovereign of Castile.

In his own recreation of the legend of the Knight of Olmedo—a hero whose life must end in violent death, as the audience knew before it entered the theater—Lope has organized the drama around the intertwined themes of love and death, those seemingly antithetical forces whose mysterious linkage has been sensed by philosophers, poets, and psychologists from Plato to Freud. As is customary in Lope,[13] the characters moved and touched by these forces are types, clear and simple in outlines, with few individualizing marks. Alonso is an unusually perfect example of the noble hero, idealistic, impractical, brave and poetic; Inés is the typical young heroine, pretty, lively, quick-witted; the King performs his usual functions as dispenser of justice and restorer of order, just as Tello fulfills the role expected of the *gracioso*—practical, materialistic, cowardly, and boastful, he is the hero's loyal servant and constant companion, even at the most intimate moments of his love affairs.[14]

The play derives its power, then, not from complexity of character and motivation but from the singular intensity and concentration, the subtle modulations and variations with which the themes of love and death are orchestrated, as well as from the all-encompassing irony that springs from the conversion into bitter reality of the graceful but worn rhetoric of the courtly lover, so often repeated throughout the drama, about the mortal wounds inflicted by love. (*El caballero de Olmedo*, to be sure, is not unique in Lope's dramatic *oeuvre* in this respect; over and over again he delights in showing how pretense, playacting, poetic fancies and conceits, lies, illusions, idle jests are transmuted into truth, a process summed up by the title of one of his plays, *Lo fingido verdadero* [*Pretense Comes True*].) No subplot distracts us from the central problem; the few characters are directly related

13. Readers interested in a general discussion of Lope's theater and its conventions—the three-act verse play, the mingling of tragic and comic, the disregard of unities of time, place, and action, the dominant themes of love, honor, religion, national glory, etc.—may consult A. G. Reichenberger, "The Uniqueness of the *comedia*," *Hispanic Review* 27 (1959): 303-316; Karl Vossler, *Lope de Vega und sein Zeitalter* (Munich: Beck, 1932); and A. A. Parker, *The Approach to the Spanish Drama of the Golden Age,* Diamante VI (London: The Hispanic and Luso-Brazilian Councils, 1957). The last study should be used with care; the argument that *all* Golden Age drama demonstrates, through the principle of poetic justice, strict adherence to Catholic Counter-Reform morality (itself interpreted narrowly) is ingenious but can be maintained only at the risk of deforming the feeling and intent of a number of plays.

14. The *gracioso*, a figure peculiar to the Spanish theater of the Golden Age, is well analyzed by José F. Montesinos in "Algunas observaciones sobre la figura del donaire en el teatro de Lope de Vega," *Estudios sobre Lope* (Madrid: Anaya, 1967). Tello, it must be added, though cowardly at night in the company of a witch (vss. 960-975), displays a somewhat atypical bravery in fighting at the side of his master (vss. 701-706) and unusual dignity of thought and expression in his final lament for his dead master (vss. 2627-2706), possibly because Lope wished to distinguish him from the despicable Sempronio of the *Celestina*.

to Alonso's life; and few lines of verse are purely decorative, nonfunctional embellishments unrelated to the furtherance of plot and theme.

Act I begins in Spanish with the word *Amor*; the time is spring, and dialogue and monologue create an atmosphere of light, life, and hope, from Alonso's description of Inés's shining beauty amidst the bustle of the fair through Inés's brief evocation of the appearance of her garden at dawn (vss. 707-710) to Fabia's promise at the end of the act that Inés will surely marry the flower of Olmedo. We may not even have noticed Alonso's early jesting comparison of himself with the criminal condemned to death (vss. 155-158) or Fabia's praise of Alonso as a new Adonis, followed so quickly by her reference to the latter's tragic death (vss. 861-862). These were, however, the opening notes of the theme of death, which will be heard as loudly in Act II as is the theme of love, even though the comic *divertissement* provided by Fabia and Tello disguised as devout religious counsellors beguiles us into forgetting the insistence of the darker theme, announced, as was love in Act I, by Alonso's opening words, "I think *death* is better, Tello, than life without seeing her"; continued in Tello's recitation of the poem about love and death (vss. 1111-1160); and confirmed by Alonso's account of the slaying of the goldfinch by the hawk (vss. 1755-1788).

These first two acts are notably devoid of the adventure, conflict, heroism, and excitement that fill so many of Lope's plays. We have seen little but the sentimental private aspect of Alonso's life. And the intimate, lyric mood has been accompanied by elastic chronology and time references.[15] But a knight of Olmedo meant to die a hero's death must be more than a languishing lover. Romeo remains primarily a private figure, even though his sense of honor and manliness have been established by his duel with Tybalt. For Lope, however, as for Aristotle, the private citizen and his affairs were never fitting subjects for grave and tragic plays. Already in Act II Alonso had been linked to national concerns when King Juan II conferred on him the habit

15. The events of Act I take place on two days and the intervening night; but it is impossible to determine how much time has elapsed between Acts I and II: Tello speaks of many trips between Olmedo and Medina (vss. 892-893), but the midnight visit to the crossroads with Fabia, projected in Act I, seems to have just taken place (vss. 599-620, 960-975); the day of the Feast of the Invention of the Cross is said to be near (vss. 1303-1306), but whether a week away or only a day or so is never clear.

of a military order (vss. 1595-1597). Act III proceeds immediately to develop this public dimension of the hero's life with Alonso's remarkable feats in the bullring before the King and an applauding multitude. Thus, when Alonso dies, the audience will sense his loss as not only a private but also a public tragedy. Now, too, in characteristic Lopean fashion, as the excitement of the action increases and as the end approaches, the brief remaining hours are counted with precision. Alonso fights in the afternoon, sees Inés after darkness has fallen, and is killed at midnight. Tello reports the murder, and sentence is pronounced on the assassins on the following day.

The theme of love, almost totally supplanted in Act III by that of death, is granted a brief reprise in the final conversation between Alonso and Inés; but even here Alonso's sense of impending doom overshadows his love. Afterward, there is no time for anything but heroism and death on a black and somber night that contrasts memorably with the bright spring day on which the action began.

The direct cause of Alonso's death is, of course, the jealousy of Rodrigo, his rival in love and arms, as it was in both the *Caballero de Olmedo* of 1606 and the *bailes* of 1615 and 1617. But Lope's tragedy invites us to speculate, as the *Celestina* does—but as the earlier treatments of the knight's story most assuredly do not—on the general problem of evil and suffering in this world. Why, in other words, should the life of an exemplary knight, of inestimable value to his family and his country, be extinguished in its prime by foul means? Is there some hidden flaw in Alonso's character, some error in moral judgment which makes him, however attractive, in some sense merit his punishment? Or has fate alone, for inscrutable reasons, maneuvered his life to a predetermined end? The answer is inescapable: despite his goodness and innocence, perhaps even because of them, Alonso is destiny's victim.[16] Alonso's moral worth is established not only

16. For contrary views, see Parker, op. cit., pp. 9-10; Alan Soons, "Towards an Interpretation of *El Caballero de Olmedo*," *Romanische Forschungen* 73 (1961): 160-168; William C. McCrary, *The Goldfinch and the Hawk: A Study of Lope de Vega's Tragedy "El Caballero de Olmedo*," University of North Carolina Studies in the Romance Languages and Literatures, No. 62 (Chapel Hill, N.C.: University of North Carolina Press, 1966). Professor Parker first, and other critics after him, have identified the principle of poetic justice as the cornerstone of Golden Age drama; it is affirmed that

by his own generous chivalrous actions but by the often stressed comparison and contrast with Calisto. In their carnal passion Calisto and Melibea sinned against the laws of their society and the dictates of the Church; but Alonso's love is chaste, his intentions firmly bent on matrimony (vss. 153, 176-177, 1891-1893, 2475-2476). Calisto sacrifices his own and Melibea's honor on the altar of his amorous desires and dies a senseless, unheroic death, denied the last rites of confession and absolution. Alonso's final journey to Olmedo is motivated by filial love and obedience; his brave but futile combat against treacherous enemies heightens his heroism, and his dying moments allow time for the last sacraments. If we seek to find some error or flaw in Alonso, it is only the one he recognizes in the brief moment of *anagnorisis* before his death: "How little credit I gave to warnings from heaven! Trust in my own valor has deceived me, and envy and jealousy have killed me" (vss. 2463-2466). In other words, Alonso, the "rationalist" who scoffs at superstition and does not believe in witchcraft, has perhaps never given sufficient weight to the control heaven exerts over all men's lives. Trusting too much in the proven strength of his own arm, ultimately frail because it is human, he attributes to human agents or psychological causes both of the warnings from heaven (the Shade and the Peasant) sent to him on that fearful night and thus disregards the central tenet of seventeenth-century belief, namely, that the supraterrestrial is with us always.

---

no character in a play of this period is ever allowed to suffer punishment of any sort—frustration, degradation, death, or damnation—without having in some measure deserved such retribution through his own moral fault or error. It is then argued that, since Alonso dies, he must have sinned. His faults are variously assumed to be illicit love, employing the dangerous witch Fabia, acquiescing in Inés's morally reprehensible sham religious vocation, and a foolish sense of honor which forces him to continue on the road to Olmedo in the face of all warnings. The most serious accusation, perhaps, concerns Alonso's use of Fabia, for it is true that the Church abhorred, and the state condemned to death, both witches and those who made use of their black arts. Alonso, however, uses Fabia as a messenger, not as a witch, and clearly proclaims his own lack of belief in the power of magic over the human will (vss. 984-987). And Fabia herself, though convinced of her own demonic powers, is a curiously benign figure who, if Alonso's own words are to be believed, has sent the Shade and the Peasant to warn him against danger. There is great danger in reading the *Caballero* as a mere repetition of the *Celestina*: time and again Lope insists that Alonso and Inés are *not* illicit lovers like Calisto and Melibea; that Tello is *not* a hypocritical coward like Sempronio; and that Fabia is *not* the malevolent force that Celestina undeniably was (see Marcel Bataillon, *La Célestine selon Fernando de Rojas* [Paris: Didier, 1961], Ch. 8).

The supraterrestrial control of Alonso's life is manifest throughout the drama. It is strongly suggested that his love itself, which arouses Rodrigo's murderous jealousy, was preordained by the stars and planets presiding over his birth (vss. 1-30, 215-228, 1723). Alonso's inexplicable melancholy, the symbolic murder of the goldfinch by the hawk, the grim Shade, the mysterious Peasant who sings the traditional verses of the *caballero*, augmented by four lines of Lope's own invention ("Shades have warned him/ not to set out," etc.)[17]—all these foreshadowings, omens, and portents, revealing as they must the intervention of another world into human affairs, are Lope's major thematic additions to the inherited legend of the Knight of Olmedo. Essentially innocent of wrongdoing, Alonso cannot but evoke pity in us because of his blindness to his approaching doom, which, however, we feel no act of his could have forestalled. In retrospect, it is clear that Alonso's star-crossed love, Fabia and her spells, Rodrigo and his jealousy are all tools utilized to fulfill the predetermined pattern of Alonso's life. Apparent chance happenings (e.g., the confusion at the garden window about Inés's green ribbon), words spoken in jest (Alonso's punning on "chapel-wedding-death," Fabia's playing on the word "Lord") are revealed in the end to have been, as E. B. O. Borgerhoff once observed with regard to Julien Sorel, "elements of an existence already disposed of, even then irrevocably spelled out."[18]

In sum, then, Lope's recreation of the legend of the Knight of Olmedo reveals an intuition of the ordering of human life, even of the lives of the pure in heart like Alonso, by forces outside our visible world and beyond our comprehension. If man's responsibility for his own fate is diminished by this conception, at least God's justice is not reduced to the level of man's puny understanding. And the strong sense of a superior order demonstrated by the use of omens, portents, and conceits and deceits converted into the truth rescues the universe from blind chaos, just as the subtly implied comparison between Christ and Alonso hidden within the play serves to indicate some unseen purpose at work in Alonso's annihilation.

---

17. Since these lines do not appear in any other treatment, in poetry or in drama, of the Knight's legend, we are forced to conclude that they are Lope's own addition to the traditional song.

18. "The Anagram in *Le Rouge et le noir*," *Modern Language Notes* 68 (1953): 386.

Alonso's death occurs, as Tello reminds us, on "the night of the festival celebrated by the knights of Medina in honor of the May Cross—so that it should indeed be true that *where there is a cross, there is passion also*" (vss. 2648-2649). King Juan II awards the Christian cross of a military order to Alonso immediately after giving his approval to the distinctive stigmata of dress imposed upon Jews and Moors (vss. 1583-1597), so that Alonso becomes by implication the defender of the Christian faith against hostile creeds. Further, he is strongly linked with the goldfinch (in the portentous vision at the close of Act II) and the phoenix (in Tello's final eulogy: Alonso's "burial will be like that of the phoenix, Sire," vss. 2700-2701), both well-known symbols of the resurrection.[19] On the night of his death, alone, without companions, Alonso is journeying toward a reunion with his father. These indications drawn from the play itself, though significant, may not seem conclusive. When combined, however, with the fact that the same *seguidilla* ("So by night they killed him") is employed in two of Lope's *autos sacramentales* (*Del pan y del palo* and the *Auto de los cantares*), in which the murdered knight is Christ and the allegory of the *autos* stirs occasional

19. Alison Turner was the first to point out this particular significance of the goldfinch symbol in the play ("The Dramatic Function of Imagery and Symbolism in *Peribáñez* and *El caballero de Olmedo*," *Symposium* 20 [1966]: 180-181). In European art from the thirteenth century on the goldfinch so frequently appears in devotional pictures in which Christ is depicted as an infant or small child, that the bird alone could on occasion be a symbol of Christ Himself; but it also carries more specific symbolic meanings related to the action of *El caballero*: it can represent the soul in opposition to the body; death and the Passion of Christ (because of the touches of red in its plumage); and the Resurrection (see Herbert Friedmann, *The Symbolic Goldfinch*, Bollingen Series, No. 7 [New York: Pantheon Books, Inc., 1946]).

20. It is not to be concluded that Lope was writing a theological drama, even to the extent that Calderón may have done so in *La vida es sueño* (*Life is a Dream*). Surely, however, the archetypical pattern of tragedy as a propitiatory sacrifice is more than usually apparent in *El caballero*. Within the Christian framework the ultimate model for such tragic action is the Passion of Christ, in which the agony of death is only the prelude to redemption and resurrection. The Christian tragedy can thus terminate, as the *Caballero* does, with a sense of relative tranquility and order restored. See Northrop Frye, *Anatomy of Criticism* (Princeton: Princeton University Press, 1957), p. 215: "Christianity, too, sees tragedy as an episode in the divine comedy, the larger scheme of redemption and resurrection. The sense of tragedy as a prelude to comedy seems almost inseparable from anything explicitly Christian. The serenity of the final double chorus in the St. Matthew Passion would hardly be attainable if composer and audience did not know that there was more to the story. Nor would the death of Samson lead to 'calm of mind, all passion spent,' if Samson were not a prototype of the rising Christ, associated at the appropriate moment with the phoenix."

echoes of the action of the secular drama, it seems legitimate to assume that Lope himself sensed some likeness between the love and death of Alonso and the passion of Christ. The destruction of the beautiful and the good in the person of Alonso is thus not an act of wanton cruelty but a sacrifice necessary within the hidden grand design of the universe.[20]

WILLARD F. KING

Bryn Mawr College

THE KNIGHT OF OLMEDO

PERSONAS

Don Alonso
Don Rodrigo
Don Fernando
Don Pedro
El Rey Don Juan II
El Condestable
Doña Inés
Doña Leonor
Ana
Fabia
Tello
Mendo
Laín
Un Labrador
Una Sombra
Criados, Acompañamiento del Rey, Gente

DRAMATIS PERSONAE

Don Alonso
Don Rodrigo
Don Fernando
Don Pedro
King Juan II
The Lord High Constable
Doña Inés
Doña Leonor
Ana
Fabia
Tello
Mendo
Laín
A Peasant
A Shade
Servants, the King's retinue, various people in crowds

ACTO PRIMERO

Sale Don Alonso.

ALONSO.   Amor, no te llame amor
el que no te corresponde,
pues que no hay materia adonde
imprima forma el favor.
Naturaleza, en rigor,   5
conservó tantas edades
correspondiendo amistades;
que no hay animal perfeto
si no asiste a su conceto
la unión de dos voluntades.   10
    De los espíritus vivos
de unos ojos procedió
este amor, que me encendió
con fuegos tan excesivos.
No me miraron altivos,   15
antes, con dulce mudanza,
me dieron tal confianza,
que, con poca diferencia,
pensando correspondencia,
engendra amor esperanza.   20
    Ojos, si ha quedado en vos
de la vista el mismo efeto,
amor vivirá perfeto,
pues fue engendrado de dos;
pero si tú, ciego dios,   25
diversas flechas tomaste,
no te alabes que alcanzaste
la vitoria, que perdiste
si de mí solo naciste,
pues imperfeto quedaste.   30

Salen Tello, *criado, y* Fabia.

---

4. *imprima forma*] 1641; *no imprima forma* H, RAE, M, B.

ACT I

[A street in Medina del Campo.]
Enter Don Alonso.

ALONSO.

Oh love, he who does not love should not speak of you, since there is then no matter on which love's favor may impress its form. In truth, nature has preserved the world down through so many ages by mutual affection, for there is no complete animal unless it be conceived by the union of two wills. This love of mine, which has kindled me with searing flames, was born from the living spirits that issued from a pair of eyes. They did not look at me haughtily; rather, with their sweet changes of expression, they gave me confidence, for when two people are alike,[1] love engenders hope in the expectation of striking an answering chord. Oh melting eyes, if you have felt the same effect from my glances, love will live fully, for it was born of two people. But, oh blind god, if you shot opposing arrows at us two, do not congratulate yourself on achieving victory. You have lost if you were born of me alone, because you have remained incomplete.[2]

Enter Tello, *a servant [of Don Alonso's], and* Fabia.

FABIA.	¿A mí forastero?
TELLO.	A ti.
FABIA.	Debe de pensar que yo soy perro de muestra.
TELLO.	No.
FABIA.	¿Tiene algún achaque?
TELLO.	Sí.
FABIA.	¿Qué enfermedad tiene?
TELLO.	Amor.

35

FABIA. Amor ¿de quién?

TELLO.   Allí está,
y él, Fabia, te informará
de lo que quiere mejor.

FABIA.   Dios guarde tal gentileza.

ALONSO. Tello, ¿es la madre?

TELLO.   La propia.   40

ALONSO. ¡Oh Fabia! ¡Oh retrato, oh copia
de cuanto naturaleza
    puso en ingenio mortal!
¡Oh peregrino dotor
y para enfermos de amor   45
Hipócrates celestial!
    Dame a besar esa mano,
honor de las tocas, gloria
    del monjil.

FABIA.   La nueva historia
de tu amor cubriera en vano   50
    vergüenza o respeto mío,
que ya en tus caricias veo
    tu enfermedad.

ALONSO.   Un deseo
es dueño de mi albedrío.

---

37. *y él*] H; *del* 1641; *El* M.
40. *propia*] H; *propria* 1641, but the pronunciation was as indicated by H in order to rhyme with *copia*.

FABIA.

Does that stranger want to speak to me?

TELLO.

Yes, he does.

FABIA.

He must think I'm some sort of bird dog or retriever to fetch and carry for him.

TELLO.

No.

FABIA.

Is he indisposed in some way?

TELLO.

Yes.

FABIA.

What sickness does he suffer from?

TELLO.

Love.

FABIA.

And whom does he love?

TELLO.

He's right over there, Fabia, and can tell you better than I can what he wants.

FABIA [*to* Don Alonso].

May God protect so gracious a gentleman.

ALONSO.

Tello, is this the old woman?

TELLO.

The very one.

ALONSO.

Oh Fabia! Oh living portrait and image of all that nature infused into mortal intelligence! Oh excellent doctor, celestial Hippocrates for those who are sick with love! Oh honor and glory of the widow's weeds, allow me to kiss your hand.

FABIA.

It is useless for you to try to hide the story of your new love out of shame or respect for me. I can already recognize your illness from your flattery.

ALONSO.

An ardent desire has enslaved my will.

FABIA.	El pulso de los amantes	55
	es el rostro. Aojado estás.	
	¿Qué has visto?	
ALONSO.	Un ángel.	
FABIA.	¿Qué más?	
ALONSO.	Dos imposibles, bastantes,	
	Fabia, a quitarme el sentido,	
	que es dejarla de querer	60
	y que ella me quiera.	
FABIA.	Ayer	
	te vi en la feria perdido	
	tras una cierta doncella,	
	que en forma de labradora	
	encubría el ser señora,	65
	no el ser tan hermosa y bella;	
	que pienso que doña Inés	
	es de Medina la flor.	
ALONSO.	Acertaste con mi amor:	
	esa labradora es	70
	fuego que me abrasa y arde.	
FABIA.	Alto has picado.	
ALONSO.	Es deseo	
	de su honor.	
FABIA.	Así lo creo.	
ALONSO.	Escucha, así Dios te guarde.	
	Por la tarde salió Inés	75
	a la feria de Medina,	
	tan hermosa, que la gente	
	pensaba que amanecía.	
	Rizado el cabello en lazos,	
	que quiso encubrir la liga,	80
	porque mal caerán las almas	
	si ven las redes tendidas.	
	Los ojos, a lo valiente,	
	iban perdonando vidas,	
	aunque dicen los que deja	85
	que es dichoso a quien la quita.	
	Las manos haciendo tretas,	
	que como juego de esgrima	

FABIA.

A lover's face reveals his illness as surely as the sick man's pulse. You are bewitched. What have you seen?

ALONSO.

An angel.

FABIA.

And what else bothers you?

ALONSO.

Two things which are impossible, each one enough to deprive me of my senses: one is to stop loving her, and the other, that she might love me.

FABIA.

Yesterday at the fair I saw you wandering entranced after a certain damsel dressed as a peasant girl; the disguise concealed her high lineage but not her beauty, for I'm sure that Doña Inés is the flower of Medina.[3]

ALONSO.

You've guessed my love. That peasant girl is the flame that consumes me.

FABIA.

You've set your sights high.

ALONSO.

I have no designs against her honor and good name.

FABIA.

I believe you.

ALONSO.

Hear my story, as you would have God's grace. Yesterday afternoon as Inés walked through Medina's fair, her beauty was so great that people thought the day had dawned. Bright bows caught up her curls, hiding the irresistible snare of her unbound hair, for men's hearts, like birds, flee from traps which are too obvious.[4] Like a daring soldier, her eyes graciously pardoned the lives of those they gazed upon, although those who were reprieved envied the fortune of those who perished. Her snow-white hands, set off by pointed cuffs,[5] moved with such light grace that she might, like a skillful

tiene tanta gracia en ellas,
que señala las heridas.   90
Las valonas esquinadas
en manos de nieve viva,
que muñecas de papel
se han de poner en esquinas.
Con la caja de la boca   95
allegaba infantería,
porque, sin ser capitán,
hizo gente por la villa.
Los corales y las perlas
dejó Inés, porque sabía   100
que las llevaban mejores
los dientes y las mejillas.
Sobre un manteo francés
una verdemar basquiña,
porque tenga en otra lengua   105
de su secreto la cifra.
No pensaron las chinelas
llevar de cuantos la miran
los ojos en los listones,
las almas en las virillas.   110
No se vio florido almendro
como toda parecía,
que del olor natural
son las mejores pastillas.
Invisible fue con ella   115
el amor, muerto de risa,
de ver, como pescador,
los simples peces que pican.
Unos prometieron sartas
y otros arracadas ricas;   120
pero en oídos de áspid
no hay arracadas que sirvan.
Cuál a su garganta hermosa
el collar de perlas finas;
pero, como toda es perla,   125
poco las perlas estima.
Yo, haciendo lengua los ojos,

119. *Unos prometieron*] R; *Unos le prometieron* 1641; *Unos le ofrecieron* H.
123. *Cuál a*] 1641; *Cual da a* H.

fencer, point to the spot where the wound would later appear. Her smiling mouth, like the regiment's drum, assembled infantrymen; without being a captain she recruited troops all over the town.[6] Pearls and corals Inés had left at home, knowing she wore better ones in her teeth and on her cheeks. A sea-green billowing skirt covered her French petticoats, so that she might keep the key to her secrets in another tongue.[7] Her slippers could not know how their ribbons carried off everyone's eyes and their straps[8] everyone's heart. No flowering almond was ever more perfect, for the best of incense is the fragrance of nature. Invisible by her side walked the god of love, convulsed with laughter, just like a fisherman watching the foolish fish nibble his bait. Some offered her necklaces and others rich earrings, but she was as deaf and deadly as the asp,[9] and there are no earrings suitable for the ears of an asp. Another offered a necklace of fine pearls for her beautiful throat, but as she herself is one great pearl, she values pearls lightly.[10] Speaking with my eyes, I offered no less than my soul for each

solamente le ofrecía
a cada cabello un alma,
a cada paso una vida. 130
Mirándome sin hablarme,
parece que me decía:
«No os vais, don Alonso, a Olmedo,
quedaos agora en Medina».
Creí mi esperanza, Fabia. 135
Salió esta mañana a misa,
ya con galas de señora,
no labradora fingida.
Si has oído que el marfil
del unicornio santigua 140
las aguas, así el cristal
de un dedo puso en la pila.
Llegó mi amor basilisco,
y salió del agua misma
templado el veneno ardiente 145
que procedió de su vista.
Miró a su hermana, y entrambas
se encontraron en la risa,
acompañando mi amor
su hermosura y mi porfía. 150
En una capilla entraron;
yo, que siguiéndolas iba,
entré imaginando bodas:
¡tanto quien ama imagina!
Vime sentenciado a muerte, 155
porque el amor me decía:
«Mañana mueres, pues hoy
te meten en la capilla.»
En ella estuve turbado:
ya el guante se me caía, 160
ya el rosario, que los ojos
a Inés iban y venían.
No me pagó mal; sospecho
que bien conoció que había
amor y nobleza en mí; 165

---

161. *ya... ojos*] RAE; *y en el Rosario, y a los ojos* 1641.

hair of her head, my life for each step she took. And she, gazing at me wordlessly, seemed to say: "Don't leave for Olmedo,[11] Don Alonso; stay a while in Medina." I believed the hope in my heart, Fabia, and stayed. This morning she came out to mass, dressed now as a highborn lady instead of as a country girl. If you have heard how the unicorn's ivory horn purifies and blesses water, exactly so did her white fingers bless the holy-water font. My basilisk love went to the font, and when I dipped my fingers in it after her, the burning poison infused by her eyes was tempered and soothed by the water.[12] She looked at her sister, and both of them burst out in a laugh heightened by her beauty and applauded by my love. They went into a chapel, and I followed them inside, already in my fantasy forming visions of a wedding. How fertile is the imagination of the lover! But then, suddenly, I saw myself sentenced to death, for love whispered to me: "Tomorrow you die, since today they've shut you in a chapel like a criminal on the eve of execution." I was confused and upset; I would drop my gloves and then my rosary, for I could not keep my eyes away from Inés. And she returned my glances; I think she recognized at once my love and my nobility, for she would not have looked at

que quien no piensa, no mira,
y mirar sin pensar, Fabia,
es de inorantes, y implica
contradición que en un ángel
faltase ciencia divina.   170
Con este engaño, en efeto,
le dije a mi amor que escriba
este papel; que si quieres
ser dichosa y atrevida
hasta ponerle en sus manos,   175
para que mi fe consiga
esperanzas de casarme,
tan en esto amor me inclina,
el premio será un esclavo,
con una cadena rica,   180
encomienda de esas tocas,
de malcasadas envidia.

FABIA.   Yo te he escuchado.

ALONSO.   Y ¿qué sientes?

FABIA.   Que a gran peligro te pones.

TELLO.   Escusa, Fabia, razones,   185
si no es que por dicha intentes,
    como diestro cirujano,
hacer la herida mortal.

FABIA.   Tello, con industria igual
pondré el papel en su mano,   190
    aunque me cueste la vida,
sin interés, porque entiendas
que, donde hay tan altas prendas,
sola yo fuera atrevida.
    Muestra el papel, que primero   195
le tengo de aderezar.

ALONSO.   ¿Con qué te podré pagar
la vida, el alma que espero,
    Fabia, de esas santas manos?

TELLO.   ¿Santas?

ALONSO.   ¿Pues no se han de hacer   200
milagros?

---

178. *tan en esto*] 1641; *Tan honesto* H.
200. *no se han*] 1641; *no, si han* H.

me if she'd not been interested. Idle glances without intention behind them, Fabia, are signs of stupidity; it would be an impossible contradiction if an angel like Inés should lack divine intelligence. Trusting in this illusion, I commanded my loving heart to write this letter. If you're lucky and daring enough to put it in her hands, so that I may have some hope of marriage (for love impels me toward that goal), I'll be your slave and give you a rich chain to adorn like the knight's cross[1 3] those widow's weeds which many an unhappily married girl longs to wear.

FABIA.

I've heard you out.

ALONSO.

So, what do you think about it?

FABIA.

I think you're putting yourself in great danger.

TELLO.

Don't waste time arguing, Fabia, unless, perhaps, you're trying your best, like one of our skillful sawbones, to make him die from the wound.

FABIA.

Tello, I'll put the letter into her hands with skill equal to that of any surgeon, even though it costs me my life. And I'll do it without selfish hope of gain, so you'll see that when the stakes are so high, I'm the only one who would dare to play the game. Show me the paper. [*Aside.*]   First of all, I must apply my special arts to it.

ALONSO.

Oh Fabia, how can I repay you for the life and soul I hope to receive from those blessed hands?

TELLO.

Blessed?

ALONSO.

Isn't that the right word if miracles are to be performed?

TELLO.	De Lucifer.
FABIA.	Todos los medios humanos
	tengo de intentar por ti,
	porque el darme esa cadena
	no es cosa que me da pena,
	mas confiada nací.
TELLO.	¿Qué te dice el memorial?
ALONSO.	Ven, Fabia, ven, madre honrada,
	porque sepas mi posada.
FABIA.	Tello.
TELLO.	Fabia.
FABIA.	No hables mal;
	que tengo cierta morena
	de estremado talle y cara.
TELLO.	Contigo me contentara,
	si me dieras la cadena.

205

210

Vanse, y salen Doña Inés *y* Doña Leonor.

INÉS.	Y todos dicen, Leonor,
	que nace de las estrellas.
LEONOR.	De manera que, sin ellas,
	¿no hubiera en el mundo amor?
INÉS.	Dime tú: si don Rodrigo
	ha que me sirve dos años,
	y su talle y sus engaños
	son nieve helada conmigo,
	y en el instante que vi
	este galán forastero,
	me dijo el alma, «Éste quiero»,
	y yo le dije, «Sea ansí»,
	¿quién concierta y desconcierta
	este amor y desamor?
LEONOR.	Tira como ciego amor,
	yerra mucho y poco acierta.
	Demás que negar no puedo,
	aunque es de Fernando amigo
	tu aborrecido Rodrigo,

215

220

225

230

210. *mal*] H; *mas* 1641.

TELLO.
Lucifer's miracles.

FABIA.
I'll try every way humanly possible for you. Your promise of the chain is no punishment for me, as it might be for a criminal; but then I was born optimistic.

TELLO.
So what do you think of her certificate of merit?

ALONSO.
Come, Fabia, come, reverend mother; I'll show you where I'm staying.

FABIA.
Tello—

TELLO.
Fabia—

FABIA [*aside to* Tello].
Don't speak ill of me. I've got a brunette wench with a fine figure and face who'd be just right for you.

TELLO.
I'd be happy even with you if you'd give me the chain. *Exeunt.*

[*A room in the house of Don Pedro in Medina.*]
Enter Doña Inés *and* Doña Leonor.

INÉS.
Everybody says, Leonor, that love is born of the stars.[14]

LEONOR.
You mean that if there weren't any stars, there'd be no love in the world?

INÉS.
Well, you tell me. Don Rodrigo has courted me for two years now, and both his appearance and his flattering words are icy cold to me; but at the very first moment I saw this handsome stranger, my heart said to me, "This is the one I love," and I replied to my heart, "So be it." Who produces this harmony of love and this discord of aversion?

LEONOR.
Love shoots his arrows like a blind man; he misses the target often and hits it seldom. Besides, I can't deny that the stranger

	por quien obligada quedo	
	a intercederte por él,	235
	que el forastero es galán.	
INÉS.	Sus ojos causa me dan	
	para ponerlos en él,	
	pues pienso que en ellos vi	
	el cuidado que me dio,	240
	para que mirase yo	
	con el que también le di.	
	Pero ya se habrá partido.	
LEONOR.	No le miro yo de suerte	
	que pueda vivir sin verte.	245

Ana, *criada.*

ANA.	Aquí, señora, ha venido	
	la Fabia, o la Fabiana.	
INÉS.	Pues ¿quién es esa mujer?	
ANA.	Una que suele vender	
	para las mejillas grana	250
	y para la cara nieve.	
INÉS.	¿Quieres tú que entre, Leonor?	
LEONOR.	En casas de tanto honor	
	no sé yo cómo se atreve,	
	que no tiene buena fama;	255
	mas ¿quién no desea ver?	
INÉS.	Ana, llama esa mujer.	
ANA.	Fabia, mi señora os llama.	

Fabia, *con una canastilla.*

FABIA.	Y ¡cómo si yo sabía	
	que me habías de llamar!	260
	¡Ay! Dios os deje gozar	
	tanta gracia y bizarría,	
	tanta hermosura y donaire;	
	que cada día que os veo	
	con tanta gala y aseo	265
	y pisar de tan buen aire,	
	os echo mil bendiciones;	
	y me acuerdo como agora	

258. *os llama*] 1641; H inserts *"Vase"* (Exit) after *llama*.

is handsome, even though my Fernando is the friend of your despised Rodrigo, so that I feel obliged to intercede for him.

INÉS.

The stranger's eyes move me to turn my eyes toward him. I think I saw in them the same unrest he stirred in me, so that my gaze should reveal to him that I share his pain. But there's no use in talking about it. He must have left Medina by now.

LEONOR.

He looked to me as if he could not live without seeing you again.

[*Enter*] Ana, *a servant.*

ANA.

Mistress, there's a woman at the door named Fabia or Fabiana.

INÉS.

Well, who is she?

ANA.

A woman who sells white powder for the face and rouge for the cheeks.

INÉS.

Do you think we should let her in, Leonor?

LEONOR.

I don't know how she dares to call at respectable houses. Her reputation's not good at all. But, who wouldn't be curious to see her?

INÉS.

Ana, tell her to come in.

ANA [*going to the door*].

Fabia, my mistress summons you.

[*Enter*] Fabia, *carrying a small basket.*

FABIA [*aside*].

How well I knew that you would receive me!—Ah, my ladies, may God grant you the enjoyment of so much grace and elegance, so much beauty and wit. Every day when I see you out walking in the street so gaily, dressed with such magnificence and care, I bless you a thousand times; and I remember as

de aquella ilustre señora
que con tantas perfecciones 270
fue la fénix de Medina,
fue el ejemplo de lealtad.
¡Qué generosa piedad
de eterna memoria digna!
¡Qué de pobres la lloramos! 275
¿A quién no hizo mil bienes?

INÉS. Dinos, madre, a lo que vienes.
FABIA. ¡Qué de huérfanas quedamos
por su muerte malograda,
la flor de las Catalinas! 280
Hoy la lloran mis vecinas,
no la tienen olvidada.
Y a mí, ¿qué bien no me hacía?
¡Qué en agraz se la llevó
la muerte! No se logró. 285
Aún cincuenta no tenía.
INÉS. No llores, madre, no llores.
FABIA. No me puedo consolar
cuando le veo llevar
a la muerte las mejores, 290
y que yo me quedo acá.
Vuestro padre, Dios le guarde,
¿está en casa?
LEONOR. Fue esta tarde
al campo.
FABIA. Tarde vendrá.
Si va a deciros verdades, 295
mozas sois, vieja soy yo.
Más de una vez me fio
don Pedro sus mocedades;
pero teniendo respeto
a la que pudre, yo hacía, 300
como quien se lo debía,
mi obligación. En efeto,
de diez mozas, no le daba
cinco.

296. *mozas*] B; *moza* 1641.

if it were only yesterday your illustrious mother, whose manifold perfections made her the phoenix of Medina, the very model of the faithful wife. What generous compassion, worthy of everlasting memory! How many of us poor souls weep for her loss! Not one of us but has enjoyed a thousand favors at her hands.

INÉS.

Tell us, good woman, why you have come here.

FABIA.

How many of us felt orphaned by her untimely death! Ah, she was the flower of all those who bear the pure name of Catherine.[15] To this day my neighbors have not forgotten her; they weep for her still. And as for me, how can I forget all the kindnesses she did me? Death snatched her away much too soon. She had not reached her prime. She wasn't even fifty when she died.

INÉS.

Don't cry, good woman, don't cry.

FABIA.

Nothing can console me when I see death carry off the best women, while I have remained here behind. And your father, may God keep him, is he at home?

LEONOR.

He went to the country this afternoon.

FABIA [*aside*].

And he'll come back too late. —We might as well talk plainly; after all, you are young girls, and I'm an old woman. More than once your father, Don Pedro, put his love affairs in my hands; but out of respect for your lamented mother, whom I owed so much to, I tried to restrain him, as I was duty bound to do. So I gave him only five of every ten girls he wanted.

INÉS.	¡Qué virtud!
FABIA.	No es poco,

que era vuestro padre un loco;   305
cuanto vía, tanto amaba.
　Si sois de su condición,
me admiro de que no estéis
enamoradas. ¿No hacéis,
niñas, alguna oración   310
para casaros?

INÉS.   No, Fabia.
Eso siempre será presto.

FABIA.　Padre que se duerme en esto,
mucho a sí mismo se agravia.
　La fruta fresca, hijas mías,   315
es gran cosa, y no aguardar
a que la venga a arrugar
la brevedad de los días.
　Cuantas cosas imagino,
dos solas, en mi opinión,   320
son buenas, viejas.

LEONOR.   ¿Y son?

FABIA.　Hija, el amigo y el vino.
　¿Veisme aquí? Pues yo os prometo
que fue tiempo en que tenía
mi hermosura y bizarría   325
más de algún galán sujeto.
　¿Quién no alababa mi brío?
¡Dichoso a quien yo miraba!
Pues ¿qué seda no arrastraba?
¡Qué gasto, qué plato el mío!   330
　Andaba en palmas, en andas.
Pues, ¡ay Dios!, si yo quería,
¿qué regalos no tenía
desta gente de hopalandas?
　Pasó aquella primavera,   335
no entra un hombre por mi casa;
que como el tiempo se pasa,
pasa la hermosura.

INÉS.   Espera,
¿qué es lo que traes aquí?

INÉS.

How virtuous you were!

FABIA.

It wasn't easy either. Your father was a real madman; he fell in love with every girl he laid eyes on. If you two are like your father, I'm surprised you're not in love. Don't you girls offer up prayers for your marriage?

INÉS.

No, Fabia. That day will come all too soon anyway.

FABIA.

Fathers who pay no attention to these matters do themselves injury. Fresh fruit, my daughters, is what's prized; we mustn't wait and let the flying days wrinkle its firm flesh. In my opinion, of all the things there are in the world, only two are good when they are old.

LEONOR.

What are they?

FABIA.

My daughter, only friends and wine. You see what I look like now, don't you? Well, I assure you that there was a time when my beauty and grace held many a young man captive. Was there anyone who did not praise my high spirits? The man I deigned to look at considered himself happy. What rustling silks I wore! How freely I spent, how elegantly I set my table! I walked in triumph and was honored everywhere. And if I wanted them, what gifts I could have had from all those fine gentlemen! But that springtime passed, and no man enters my house now, for as time passes, so does beauty.

INÉS.

Wait a minute. What do you have there in your basket?

FABIA.   Niñerías que vender   340
            para comer, por no hacer
            cosas malas.

LEONOR.   Hazlo ansí,
            madre, y Dios te ayudará.

FABIA.   Hija, mi rosario y misa:
            esto cuando estoy de prisa,   345
            que si no . . .

INÉS.   Vuélvete acá.
            ¿Qué es esto?

FABIA.   Papeles son
            de alcanfor y solimán.
            Aquí secretos están
            de gran consideración   350
            para nuestra enfermedad
            ordinaria.

LEONOR.   Y esto ¿qué es?

FABIA.   No lo mires, aunque estés
            con tanta curiosidad.

LEONOR.   ¿Qué es, por tu vida?

FABIA.   Una moza   355
            se quiere, niñas, casar;
            mas acertóla a engañar
            un hombre de Zaragoza.
            Hase encomendado a mí,
            soy piadosa. . . y, en fin, es   360
            limosna, porque después
            vivan en paz.

INÉS.   ¿Qué hay aquí?

FABIA.   Polvos de dientes, jabones
            de manos, pastillas, cosas
            curiosas y provechosas.   365

INÉS.   ¿Y esto?

FABIA.   Algunas oraciones.
            ¡Qué no me deben a mí
            las ánimas!

INÉS!   Un papel
            hay aquí.

354. *con tanta curiosidad*] H; *contenta curiosidad* 1641.
357. *acertóla*] H; *acertosa* 1641.

FABIA.

Childish trifles that I sell in order to buy food. Better that than
to do sinful things to earn a living.

LEONOR.

You're right, good woman. Live virtuously and God will help
you.

FABIA.

Daughter, here are my rosary and missal. They serve for my
devotions when I'm pressed for time, for when I'm not—

[*She turns to go.*]

INÉS.

Come back here. What's this?

FABIA.

Packets of camphor and sublimate.[16] And here are some secret
remedies of great value for women's monthly sickness.

LEONOR.

And this? What is it?

FABIA.

Don't look at it, even though you're bursting with curiosity.

LEONOR.

What is it, for heaven's sake?

FABIA.

There's a girl who wants to get married, my children; but a man
from Zaragoza succeeded in deflowering her. She's put herself
in my hands. I'm sorry for her and, after all, it's a charitable act,
for this way, with my help, she and her husband can live in
peace.[17]

INÉS.

What do you have here?

FABIA.

Powder for the teeth, soap for the hands, perfume tablets, and
other strange and helpful things.

INÉS.

And this?

FABIA.

Some prayers for the dead. What a lot the souls in purgatory
owe me!

INÉS.

There's a piece of paper here.

FABIA.	Diste con él,	
	cual si fuera para ti.	370
	Suéltale; no le has de ver,	
	bellaquilla, curiosilla.	
INÉS.	¡Deja, madre!	
FABIA.	Hay en la villa	
	cierto galán bachiller	
	que quiere bien una dama;	375
	prométeme una cadena	
	porque le dé yo, con pena	
	de su honor, recato y fama.	
	Aunque es para casamiento,	
	no me atrevo. Haz una cosa	380
	por mí, doña Inés hermosa,	
	que es discreto pensamiento.	
	Respóndeme a este papel,	
	y diré que me la ha dado	
	su dama.	
INÉS.	Bien lo has pensado,	385
	si pescas, Fabia, con él	
	la cadena prometida.	
	Yo quiero hacerte este bien.	
FABIA.	Tantos los cielos te den,	
	que un siglo alarguen tu vida.	390
	Lee el papel.	
INÉS.	Allá dentro,	
	y te traeré la respuesta.	*Vase.*
LEONOR.	¡Qué buena invención!	
FABIA.	¡Apresta,	
	fiero habitador del centro,	
	fuego accidental que abrase	395
	el pecho desta doncella!	

Salen Don Rodrigo *y* Don Fernando.

RODRIGO.	Hasta casarme con ella,	
	será forzoso que pase	
	por estos inconvenientes.	
FERNANDO.	Mucho ha de sufrir quien ama.	400
RODRIGO.	Aquí tenéis vuestra dama.	
FABIA.	¡Oh necios impertinentes!	
	¿Quién os ha traído aquí?	

FABIA.

Ah, you smelled it out, just as if it were meant for you. Put it back, you mustn't see it, you snoopy little rascal.

INÉS.

Oh, let me see it!

FABIA.

There's a certain young gentleman in town, a university student, who has fallen in love with a young lady; he's promised me a golden chain to give her that note, at the risk of damaging her honor, modesty, and reputation. And I don't dare to do it, even though his intentions are honorable and he wants to marry her. Do just one thing for me, my lovely lady Inés, for I've had a clever idea. Answer the note for me, and I'll tell him that his lady has sent the message to him.

INÉS.

You've planned it well, Fabia, if you manage to reel in the promised chain with my message. I'd like to do you that favor.

FABIA.

May heaven favor you so richly that you live a hundred years. Read the note.

INÉS.

I'll take it to my room and bring you the answer later.

Exit [Doña Inés].

LEONOR.

What a clever thought!

FABIA [*aside*].

Oh savage denizen of the earth's core, prepare the flames of passion[18] to burn this maiden's breast!

Enter Don Rodrigo *and* Don Fernando.

RODRIGO [*to* Don Fernando].

Until we are married, I'll have to put up with these bothersome obstacles.

FERNANDO.

Lovers have to bear a lot.

RODRIGO.

Your mistress Leonor is here.

FABIA [*aside*].

Oh troublesome fools! Who brought you here?

RODRIGO. Pero ¡en lugar de la mía,
          aquella sombra!
FABIA.   Sería   405
          gran limosna para mí,
          que tengo necesidad.
LEONOR.   Yo haré que os pague mi hermana.
FERNANDO. Si habéis tomado, señora,
          o por ventura os agrada   410
          algo de lo que hay aquí,
          si bien serán cosas bajas
          las que aquí puede traer
          esta venerable anciana,
          pues no serán ricas joyas   415
          para ofreceros la paga,
          mandadme que os sirva yo.
LEONOR.   No habemos comprado nada;
          que es esta buena mujer
          quien suele lavar en casa   420
          la ropa.
RODRIGO.   ¿Qué hace don Pedro?
LEONOR.   Fue al campo, pero ya tarda.
RODRIGO. ¿Mi señora doña Inés?
LEONOR.   Aquí estaba; pienso que anda
          despachando esta mujer.   425
RODRIGO. Si me vio por la ventana,
          ¿quién duda que huyó por mí?
          ¿Tanto de ver se recata
          quien más servirla desea?

                Salga Doña Inés.

LEONOR.   Ya sale. Mira que aguarda   430
          por la cuenta de la ropa
          Fabia.
INÉS.   Aquí la traigo, hermana.
          Tomad y haced que ese mozo
          la lleve.
FABIA.   ¡Dichosa el agua
          que ha de lavar, doña Inés,   435
          las reliquias de la holanda
          que tales cristales cubre!

RODRIGO.

But my lady's place is taken by that ghoulish figure!

FABIA [*to* Doña Leonor].

That would be a great kindness to me, for I'm very poor.

LEONOR.

I'll have my sister pay you.

FERNANDO.

My lady, if you've selected anything from this woman's wares, or if perchance you see something that you like, allow me to make you a present of it, though in truth the things this venerable old woman carries around must be poor cheap trinkets and not the rich jewels I would offer you.

LEONOR.

We've bought nothing. This good woman washes clothes for us.

RODRIGO.

What is Don Pedro doing?

LEONOR.

He went to the country; but it's past time for him to return.

RODRIGO.

And Doña Inés?

LEONOR.

She was here a moment ago. I think she's busy attending to this old woman.

RODRIGO [*aside*].

She must have seen me coming as she looked out the window. She's bound to have run away to avoid me. —Does she shrink so modestly from seeing the man who most fervently desires to serve her?

Enter Doña Inés [*with a piece of paper in her hand*].

LEONOR.

She's coming back now. [*To* Doña Inés.] Don't forget that Fabia is waiting for the laundry list.

INÉS.

I've got it here, sister. Take it, Fabia, and have that boy carry the clothes for you.

FABIA.

Oh happy the water, Doña Inés, that will wash the traces of your presence from the linen that covers such fragile limbs!

Lea.

Seis camisas, diez toallas,
cuatro tablas de manteles,
dos cosidos de almohadas,   440
seis camisas de señor,
ocho sábanas... Mas basta,
que todo vendrá más limpio
que los ojos de la cara.

RODRIGO. Amiga, ¿queréis feriarme   445
ese papel, y la paga
fiad de mí, por tener
de aquellas manos ingratas
letra siquiera en las mías?

FABIA. ¡En verdad que negociara   450
muy bien si os diera el papel!
Adiós, hijas de mi alma.   *Vase.*

RODRIGO. Esta memoria aquí había
de quedar, que no llevarla.

INÉS. Llévala y vuélvela, a efeto   455
de saber si algo le falta.
Mi padre ha venido ya.
Vuesas mercedes se vayan
o le visiten, que siente
que nos hablen, aunque calla.   460

RODRIGO. Para sufrir el desdén
que me trata desta suerte,
pido al amor y a la muerte
que algún remedio me den.
Al amor, porque también   465
puede templar tu rigor
con hacerme algún favor;
y a la muerte, porque acabe
mi vida; pero no sabe
la muerte, ni quiere amor.   470
Entre la vida y la muerte,
no sé qué medio tener,
pues amor no ha de querer
que con tu favor acierte;
y siendo fuerza quererte,   475

(*She reads.*)   Six chemises, ten towels, four tablecloths, two
pillow cases, six men's shirts, eight sheets. —But we need talk no
more of it; everything will come back as clean as the driven
snow.

RODRIGO.

Good woman, will you sell me that piece of paper? You can
trust me to pay for it, so I may at least hold a few words
written by those ungrateful hands in my own.

FABIA.

I would certainly be doing a fine bit of business if I gave you
this piece of paper! Goodbye, dear girls.   *Exit* [Fabia].

RODRIGO.

That list should stay here; she shouldn't be taking if off.

INÉS.

She takes it away with her and then brings it back so she'll
know if anything is missing. My father has come now. You
gentlemen should either leave or visit with him; he doesn't like
for people to talk to us even though he doesn't say anything
about it.

RODRIGO.

I pray to love and death that they may give me the strength to
bear the scorn with which I am treated. I pray to love, because
it may also temper your cruelty and grant me a favor from you;
and to death, in the hope that it may end my life. But death
cannot, and love will not. Caught between life and death, I
know not what middle course to take. Love does not choose
that I should find the way to your favor; and since I can do no

quire el amor que te pida
que seas tú mi homicida.
Mata, ingrata, a quien te adora:
serás mi muerte, señora,
pues no quieres ser mi vida.   480
Cuanto vive, de amor nace
y se sustenta de amor;
cuanto muere, es un rigor
que nuestras vidas deshace.
Si al amor no satisface   485
mi pena, ni la hay tan fuerte
con que la muerte me acierte,
debo de ser inmortal,
pues no me hacen bien ni mal
ni la vida ni la muerte.   *Vanse los dos.*   490

INÉS.   ¡Qué de necedades juntas!
LEONOR.   No fue la tuya menor.
INÉS.   ¿Cuándo fue discreto amor,
    si del papel me preguntas?
LEONOR.   ¿Amor te obliga a escribir   495
    sin saber a quién?
INÉS.   Sospecho
    que es invención que se ha hecho,
    para probarme a rendir,
    de parte del forastero.
LEONOR.   Yo también lo imaginé.   500
INÉS.   Si fue ansí, discreto fue.
    Leerte unos versos quiero.

Lea.

«Yo vi la más hermosa labradora,
en la famosa feria de Medina,
que ha visto el sol adonde más se inclina   505
desde la risa de la blanca aurora.

482-484. *y se ... deshace*] *y se sustenta de amor/ cuanto muere, es un rigor,/ que
nuestras vidas deshace* 1641; *de amor/ cuanto muere: es* H; *de amor: cuanto muere es*
RAE, B, R. The change in punctuation alters the sense slightly; any of the modern
punctuations is possible within the context.

less than love you, love must desire that I beg you to kill me. Slay then, oh my ungrateful love, the one who adores you; you shall be my death, my lady, for you will not be my life. All things that live are born of love; and all things that die, perish from the harsh disdain that undoes their lives.[19] If my anguish neither satisfies the demands of love nor is strong enough to bring my death, I must be immortal, for neither death nor life can kill or save me. *Exeunt* [Don Rodrigo *and* Don Fernando].

INÉS.

What a string of nonsense!

LEONOR.

You were no less foolish.

INÉS.

If you're talking about the message, when was love ever discreet?

LEONOR.

Don't tell me love obliges you to write to an unknown person.

INÉS.

I suspect that all this was a trick invented by the handsome stranger to try to win me over.

LEONOR.

That's what I thought too.

INÉS.

And if that's what he has done, he was indeed clever. I'd like to read you a poem. (*Reads.*)

While wandering through Medina's famous fair,
I saw the loveliest of peasant maids
On whom the sun has ever cast his gaze
From dawn's pale glow to where he shines most bright.

Una chinela de color, que dora
de una coluna hermosa y cristalina
la breve basa, fue la ardiente mina
que vuela el alma a la región que adora.   510
Que una chinela fuese vitoriosa,
siendo los ojos del amor enojos,
confesé por hazaña milagrosa.
Pero díjele, dando los despojos:
"Si matas con los pies, Inés hermosa,   515
¿qué dejas para el fuego de tus ojos?"»

LEONOR.   Este galán, doña Inés,
te quiere para danzar.

INÉS.   Quiere en los pies comenzar
y pedir manos después.   520

LEONOR.   ¿Qué respondiste?

INÉS.   Que fuese
esta noche por la reja
del güerto.

LEONOR.   ¿Quién te aconseja,
o qué desatino es ése?

INÉS.   No para hablarle.

LEONOR.   Pues ¿qué?   525

INÉS.   Ven conmigo y lo sabrás.

LEONOR.   Necia y atrevida estás.

INÉS.   ¿Cuándo el amor no lo fue?

LEONOR.   Huir de amor cuando empieza.

---

525. *No para*] 1641; *No es para* H.

A colored slipper, brief and golden base
Of the slender, crystal pillar of a leg
Was burning charge enough to lift my soul
From earth to Venus' sphere of ardent love.

Confess I must that it was passing strange
To find a slipper victor in the war of love
When eyes were always thought the surest weapon.

Therefore I said to her, admitting my defeat,
"Oh, fair Inés, if feet inflict such pain,
What torture's left for arrows from your eyes?"

LEONOR.
Inés, that young man wants you for a dancing partner.
INÉS.
He wants to begin humbly with my feet and ask for my hand
later.
LEONOR.
What did you answer?
INÉS.
I told him he should come to the grating in the garden wall
tonight.
LEONOR.
Who ever suggested you should do that? Or is this madness your
own idea?
INÉS.
I have no intention of talking to him.
LEONOR.
Well, what's the purpose of this summons then?
INÉS.
Come with me and you'll find out.
LEONOR.
You're foolish and too bold.
INÉS.
Love is always that way.
LEONOR.
One should flee from love at the very first moment.

INÉS.	Nadie del primero huye,	530
	porque dicen que le influye	
	la misma naturaleza.	*Vanse.*

Salen Don Alonso, Tello y Fabia.

FABIA.	¡Cuatro mil palos me han dado!	
TELLO.	¡Lindamente negociaste!	
FABIA.	¿Si tú llevaras los medios?	535
ALONSO.	Ello ha sido disparate	
	que yo me atreviese al cielo.	
TELLO.	Y que Fabia fuese el ángel	
	que al infierno de los palos	
	cayese por levantarte.	540
FABIA.	¡Ay, pobre Fabia!	
TELLO.	¿Quién fueron	
	los crueles sacristanes	
	del facistol de tu espalda?	
FABIA.	Dos lacayos y tres pajes.	
	Allá he dejado las tocas	545
	y el monjil hecho seis partes.	
ALONSO.	Eso, madre, no importara,	
	si a tu rostro venerable	
	no se hubieran atrevido.	
	¡Oh, qué necio fui en fiarme	550
	de aquellos ojos traidores,	
	de aquellos falsos diamantes,	
	niñas que me hicieron señas	
	para engañarme y matarme!	
	Yo tengo justo castigo.	555
	Toma este bolsillo, madre;	
	y ensilla, Tello, que a Olmedo	
	nos hemos de ir esta tarde.	
TELLO.	¿Cómo, si anochece ya?	
ALONSO.	Pues ¡qué! ¿quieres que me mate?	560
FABIA.	No te aflijas, moscatel,	
	ten ánimo, que aquí trae	
	Fabia tu remedio. Toma.	

INÉS.

No one flees from his first love; nature herself, they say, gives
birth to it.[20]   *Exeunt.*

[*A room in an inn in Medina.*]
Enter Don Alonso, Tello, *and* Fabia.

FABIA.

They beat me most cruelly—four thousand blows on my poor
back!

TELLO.

What a fine mess you've made of things!

FABIA.

And if you'd been handling the affair?

ALONSO.

It was madness for me to dare to court heaven itself.

TELLO.

And to send Fabia as the angel who might raise you up to
heaven by falling into that inferno of blows.

FABIA.

Oh miserable Fabia!

TELLO.

Who were the cruel sextons who beat out the rhythm on the
choir desk of your back?[21]

FABIA.

Two lackeys and three page boys. I left my veil and weeds
there, ripped to shreds.

ALONSO.

That wouldn't matter, good mother, if they had spared your
venerable face. Oh, what a fool I was to trust those treacherous
eyes, those false diamonds, those sparkling pupils which enticed
me only to deceive and kill me! I have my just punishment.
Take this purse, good mother, and saddle my horse, Tello. We
must return to Olmedo this afternoon.

TELLO.

What do you mean? It's growing dark already.

ALONSO.

What would you have me do? Do you want me to kill myself?

FABIA.

Don't get upset, you silly boy. Take heart. Fabia has the right
medicine for you here. Take it.

ALONSO.	¡Papel!
FABIA.	Papel.
ALONSO.	No me engañes.
FABIA.	Digo que es suyo, en respuesta 565
	de tu amoroso romance.
ALONSO.	Hinca, Tello, la rodilla.
TELLO.	Sin leer no me lo mandes,
	que aun temo que hay palos dentro,
	pues en mondadientes caben. 570
ALONSO.	(*Lea.*) «Cuidadosa de saber si sois quien

presumo, y deseando que lo seáis, os suplico que
vais esta noche a la reja del jardín desta casa,
donde hallaréis atado el listón verde de las
chinelas, y ponéosle mañana en el sombrero
para que os conozca».

FABIA.	¿Qué te dice?
ALONSO.	Que no puedo
	pagarte ni encarecerte
	tanto bien.
TELLO.	Ya desta suerte
	no hay que ensillar para Olmedo.
	¿Oyen, señores rocines? 575
	Sosiéguense, que en Medina
	nos quedamos.
ALONSO.	La vecina
	noche, en los últimos fines
	con que va espirando el día,
	pone los helados pies. 580
	Para la reja de Inés
	aún importa bizarría,
	que podría ser que amor
	la llevase a ver tomar
	la cinta. Voyme a mudar. *Vase.* 585
TELLO.	Y yo a dar a mi señor,
	Fabia, con licencia tuya,
	aderezo de sereno.
FABIA.	Detente.
TELLO.	Eso fuera bueno
	a ser la condición suya 590
	para vestirse sin mí.

ALONSO.

A note!

FABIA.

A note.

ALONSO.

Don't make fun of me.

FABIA.

I tell you it's yours; it's an answer to your love poem.

ALONSO.

Down on your knees, Tello.

TELLO.

Don't make me do that until you've read it. I'm still afraid.
Words can break one's bones as well as sticks and stones.[22]

ALONSO (*reads*).

"Curious to know if you are the man I think you are—and in
the hope that you are—I beg you to come tonight to the grating
in the garden wall of my house, to which you will find the green
ribbon from my slippers tied. Put it on your hat tomorrow so I
may recognize you."

FABIA.

What does she say?

ALONSO.

Things so wonderful I can neither repay you for them nor
properly praise their worth.

TELLO.

In that case there's no need to saddle up for Olmedo. Do you
hear that, my fine horses? Settle down; we're staying in Medina.

ALONSO.

The onrushing night is setting its icy feet on those last limits
where the day is dying. Still, I must dress with care to go to
Inés's window.[23] Love might bring her out to see me pick up
the ribbon. I'm going to change. *Exit* [Don Alonso].

TELLO.

With your permission, Fabia, I'll take my leave also to dress my
master for the evening dew.

FABIA.

Stay a while.

TELLO.

I'd certainly do that if my master's nature were such that he
could get dressed without me.

FABIA.	Pues bien le puedes dejar,
	porque me has de acompañar.
TELLO.	¿A ti, Fabia?
FABIA.	A mí.
TELLO.	¿Yo?
FABIA.	Sí,

que importa a la brevedad   595
deste amor.

TELLO.   ¿Qué es lo que quieres?
FABIA.   Con los hombres, las mujeres
llevamos seguridad.
Una muela he menester
del salteador que ahorcaron   600
ayer.
TELLO.   Pues ¿no le enterraron?
FABIA.   No.
TELLO.   Pues ¿qué quieres hacer?
FABIA.   Ir por ella, y que conmigo
vayas sólo a acompañarme.
TELLO.   Yo sabré muy bien guardarme   605
de ir a esos pasos contigo.
¿Tienes seso?
FABIA.   Pues, gallina,
adonde yo voy, ¿no irás?
TELLO.   Tú, Fabia, enseñada estás
a hablar al diablo.
FABIA.   Camina.   610
TELLO.   Mándame a diez hombres juntos
temerario acuchillar,
y no me mandes tratar
en materia de difuntos.

---

604. *solo a acompañarme*] H; *solo acompañarme* 1641.

FABIA.

Well, you'll have to leave him alone anyway because you've got to come with me.

TELLO.

With you, Fabia?

FABIA.

With me.

TELLO.

Me?

FABIA.

Yes, you, if you want to speed up this love affair.

TELLO.

What do you want?

FABIA.

Women feel safer with a man around; and I need a tooth from the highwayman they hanged yesterday.[24]

TELLO.

But didn't they bury him?

FABIA.

No.

TELLO.

Well, what do you want to do?

FABIA.

I want to go and pull it out, and you need only go along with me.

TELLO.

I've got enough sense to stay away from any such excursion with you. Are you in your right mind?

FABIA.

You chicken-hearted man. Are you refusing to go where a poor old woman like me goes?

TELLO.

But, Fabia, you're trained in the art of dealing with the devil.

FABIA.

March.

TELLO.

Command me to make a bold attack with my sword against ten men all together, but don't ask me to have anything to do with the dead.

FABIA.   Si no vas, tengo de hacer   615
            que él propio venga a buscarte.
TELLO.   ¡Que tengo de acompañarte!
            ¿Eres demonio o mujer?
FABIA.   Ven, llevarás la escalera,
            que no entiendes destos casos.   620
TELLO.   Quien sube por tales pasos,
            Fabia, el mismo fin espera.

Salen Don Fernando *y* Don Rodrigo, *en hábito de noche.*

FERNANDO.   ¿De qué sirve inútilmente
            venir a ver esta casa?
RODRIGO.   Consuélase entre estas rejas,   625
            don Fernando, mi esperanza.
            Tal vez sus hierros guarnece
            cristal de sus manos blancas;
            donde las pone de día,
            pongo yo de noche el alma;   630
            que cuanto más doña Inés
            con sus desdenes me mata,
            tanto más me enciende el pecho:
            así su nieve me abrasa.
            ¡Oh rejas, enternecidas   635
            de mi llanto, quién pensara
            que un ángel endureciera
            quien vuestros hierros ablanda!
            ¡Oíd! ¿Qué es lo que está aquí?
FERNANDO.   En ellos mismos atada   640
            está una cinta o listón.
RODRIGO.   Sin duda las almas atan
            a estos hierros, por castigo
            de los que su amor declaran.
FERNANDO.   Favor fue de mi Leonor;   645
            tal vez por aquí me habla.

---

622. *espera*] The scene changes here, but 1641 does not indicate an exit; H does.

FABIA.

If you don't come with me, I'll have to send the dead man himself to look for you.

TELLO.

Then I really must go with you? Are you a woman or a devil?

FABIA.

Come on. You can carry the ladder, because you don't know anything about these affairs.

TELLO.

Anybody who seeks to rise by such evil means, Fabia, must expect the highwayman's fate in the end.

[*Exeunt.*]

[*Street and exterior view of Don Pedro's house and garden wall.*]
Enter Don Rodrigo *and* Don Fernando, *dressed for the evening.*[25]

FERNANDO.

What's the use in coming to gaze upon this house?

RODRIGO.

My loving hope receives some solace from this grating. Now and again the fragile crystal of her white hands graces these iron bars, and where she has put her hands by day, I put my soul by night; for the more cruelly Doña Inés disdains me, the more she kindles the fire of love in my breast, because her icy scorn burns my soul. Oh you gratings, moved to pity by my tears, who would believe that the man who softens your iron could harden the heart of an angel! But look! What's this here?

FERNANDO.

A ribbon or a strip of cloth is tied to the grating.

RODRIGO.

No doubt, just as confessed criminals are put in chains, they punish those who confess their love by tying their souls to these iron bars.

FERNANDO.

I think it's a token of love from my Leonor; sometimes she talks to me here.

RODRIGO. Que no lo será de Inés
dice mi desconfianza;
pero, en duda de que es suyo,
porque sus manos ingratas 650
pudieron ponerle acaso,
basta que la fe me valga.
Dadme el listón.
FERNANDO. No es razón,
si acaso Leonor pensaba
saber mi cuidado ansí, 655
y no me le ve mañana.
RODRIGO. Un remedio se me ofrece.
FERNANDO. ¿Cómo?
RODRIGO. Partirle.
FERNANDO. ¿A qué causa?
RODRIGO. A que las dos nos le vean,
y sabrán con esta traza 660
que habemos venido juntos.
FERNANDO. Gente por la calle pasa.

Salen Don Alonso *y* Tello, *de noche.*

TELLO. Llega de presto a la reja;
mira que Fabia me aguarda
para un negocio que tiene 665
de grandísima importancia.
ALONSO. ¡Negocio Fabia esta noche
contigo!
TELLO. Es cosa muy alta.
ALONSO. ¿Cómo?
TELLO. Yo llevo escalera,
y ella...
ALONSO. ¿Qué lleva?
TELLO. Tenazas. 670

663-666. *Llega ... importancia*] 1641 erroneously gives these lines to Rodrigo; H
corrects as here.

RODRIGO.

My despairing heart tells me it can't be a token of love from Inés; but my faith helps me to sustain the saving doubt that it is hers, for her ungrateful hands could by chance have placed it here. Give me the ribbon.

FERNANDO.

That's not fair. Leonor may have thought she'd discover my feelings for her in this way; and if you take it, she won't see me wearing her ribbon tomorrow.

RODRIGO.

I've got a solution.

FERNANDO.

What?

RODRIGO.

We'll divide it.

FERNANDO.

What for?

RODRIGO.

So that both of the girls may see us wearing the ribbon, and that way they'll know we came together.

[*They divide the ribbon.*]

FERNANDO.

Somebody's coming down this street.

Enter Don Alonso *and* Tello, *dressed for the evening.*²⁶

TELLO [*to* Don Alonso].

Hurry to the grating. Fabia is waiting for me to help her in an affair of the greatest importance.

ALONSO.

Fabia has got some sort of business with you tonight!

TELLO.

It's a very lofty matter.

ALONSO.

What do you mean?

TELLO.

I'm carrying the ladder, and she—

ALONSO.

What's she carrying?

TELLO.

The pincers.

ALONSO.	Pues ¿qué habéis de hacer?
TELLO.	Sacar
	una dama de su casa.
ALONSO.	Mira lo que haces, Tello;
	no entres adonde no salgas.
TELLO.	No es nada, por vida tuya.
ALONSO.	Una doncella ¿no es nada?
TELLO.	Es la muela del ladrón
	que ahorcaron ayer.
ALONSO.	Repara
	en que acompañan la reja
	dos hombres.
TELLO.	¿Si están de guarda?
ALONSO.	¡Qué buen listón!
TELLO.	Ella quiso
	castigarte.
ALONSO.	¿No buscara,
	si fui atrevido, otro estilo?
	Pues advierta que se engaña.
	Mal conoce a don Alonso,
	que por excelencia llaman
	el caballero de Olmedo.
	¡Vive Dios, que he de mostrarla
	a castigar de otra suerte
	a quien la sirve!
TELLO.	No hagas
	algún disparate.
ALONSO.	Hidalgos,
	en las rejas de esa casa
	nadie se arrima.
RODRIGO.	¿Qué es esto?
FERNANDO.	Ni en el talle ni en el habla
	conozco este hombre.
RODRIGO.	¿Quién es
	el que con tanta arrogancia
	se atreve a hablar?
ALONSO.	El que tiene
	por lengua, hidalgos, la espada.

Line numbers in margin: 675, 680, 685, 690, 695

ALONSO.

Well, what do the two of you have to do?

TELLO.

We're going to extract a lady from her house.[27]

ALONSO.

Be careful what you do, Tello; don't get into something you can't get out of.

TELLO.

It's nothing, I swear.

ALONSO.

A young lady isn't anything?

TELLO.

It's the back tooth of the thief they hanged yesterday.

ALONSO.

Look! Two men are standing by the grating.

TELLO.

Do you suppose they're on guard?

ALONSO.

What a fine ribbon she's left for me!

TELLO.

She wanted to punish you.

ALONSO.

Don't you think she might have looked for another way to do it if I was too bold? Well, she'd better understand she's made a mistake. She underestimates the Don Alonso they call the "Knight of Olmedo" for his merit. By heaven, I'll teach her to punish those who serve her some other way!

TELLO.

Don't do anything foolish.

ALONSO.

Gentlemen, nobody may loiter near the windows of this house.

RODRIGO [*aside to* Don Fernando].

What's this?

FERNANDO.

I don't recognize this man either by his figure or his speech.

RODRIGO.

Who dares to speak so arrogantly?

ALONSO.

A man whose sword speaks for him, gentlemen.

RODRIGO.	Pues hallará quien castigue	
	su locura temeraria.	700
TELLO.	Cierra, señor, que no son	
	muelas que a difuntos sacan.	
		Retírenlos.
ALONSO.	No los sigas, bueno está.	
TELLO.	Aquí se quedó una capa.	
ALONSO.	Cógela y ven por aquí,	705
	que hay luces en las ventanas.	

Salen Doña Leonor *y* Doña Inés.

INÉS.	Apenas la blanca Aurora,	
	Leonor, el pie de marfil	
	puso en las flores de abril,	
	que pinta, esmalta y colora,	710
	cuando a mirar el listón	
	salí, de amor desvelada,	
	y con la mano turbada	
	di sosiego al corazón.	
	En fin, él no estaba allí.	715
LEONOR.	Cuidado tuvo el galán.	
INÉS.	No tendrá los que me dan	
	sus pensamientos a mí.	
LEONOR.	Tú, que fuiste el mismo yelo,	
	¿en tan breve tiempo estás	720
	de esa suerte?	
INÉS.	No sé más	
	de que me castiga el cielo.	
	O es venganza o es vitoria	
	de amor en mi condición:	
	parece que el corazón	725
	se me abrasa en su memoria.	
	Un punto sólo no puedo	
	apartarla dél. ¿Qué haré?	

Sale Don Rodrigo, *con el listón en el sombrero.*

---

702. *sacan*] 1641 inserts *retírenlos* after vs. 703; H sensibly relocates the direction as here.

706. *ventanas*] Although the scene must change here, 1641 does not indicate an exit; H does.

717. *tendrá*] 1641; *tendrán* H.

RODRIGO.

Well, he'll find someone to punish his rash folly.

TELLO.

Attack him, master. This is not the same sort of thing as extracting teeth from dead men.

They drive Don Fernando *and* Don Rodrigo *off.*

ALONSO.

Don't go after them. That's enough.

TELLO.

One of them left his cape here.

ALONSO.

Pick it up and come this way. There are lights in the windows.

[*Exeunt.*]

[*A room in Don Pedro's house.*]
Enter Doña Leonor *and* Doña Inés.

INÉS.

Oh Leonor, the white dawn had scarcely set her ivory foot on the April flowers which she paints with bright enamels when I came out, sleepless from love, to look for the ribbon. Feeling the grating with my unsteady hand, I gave peace to my heart. The ribbon was not there.

LEONOR.

The young man is interested in you.

INÉS.

He can't be as concerned as the thought of him has made me.

LEONOR.

How can it be that you, who were ice itself, have come to be like this in so short a time!

INÉS.

I can only think that heaven is punishing me. It's either the vengeance or the victory of love against me; my heart seems to catch fire when I think of him. Not for an instant can I put him out of my mind. What shall I do?

Enter Don Rodrigo, *with the ribbon on his hat.*

RODRIGO. (Nunca, amor, imaginé
            que te sujetara el miedo.   730
            Ánimo para vivir;
            que aquí está Inés.) Al señor
            don Pedro busco.
INÉS.   Es error
            tan de mañana acudir,
            que no estará levantado.   735
RODRIGO. Es un negocio importante.
INÉS.   No he visto tan necio amante.
LEONOR.   Siempre es discreto lo amado
            y necio lo aborrecido.
RODRIGO. ¡Que de ninguna manera   740
            puedo agradar una fiera
            ni dar memoria a su olvido!
INÉS.   ¡Ay, Leonor! No sin razón
            viene don Rodrigo aquí,
            si yo misma le escribí   745
            que fuese por el listón.
LEONOR.   Fabia este engaño te ha hecho.
INÉS.   Presto romperé el papel,
            que quiero vengarme en él
            de haber dormido en mi pecho.   750

       Salen Don Pedro, *su padre, y* Don Fernando.

FERNANDO. Hame puesto por tercero
            para tratarlo con vos.
PEDRO.   Pues hablaremos los dos
            en el concierto primero.
FERNANDO. Aquí está, que siempre amor   755
            es reloj anticipado.
PEDRO.   Habréle Inés concertado
            con la llave del favor.
FERNANDO. De lo contrario se agravia.

750. *de haber dormido*] H; *de ha dormido* 1641.

RODRIGO [*aside*].
Never did I imagine, love, that fear would hold you back. May God grant me courage to live, for Inés is here. —I've come to see Don Pedro.

INÉS.
It's a mistake to come so early in the morning. He won't be up yet.

RODRIGO.
It's an important matter.

INÉS [*aside to* Doña Leonor].
I've never seen such a stupid lover.

LEONOR.
Those we love are always discreet, and those we abhor are always stupid.

RODRIGO [*aside*].
Is there no way for me to please this cruel creature or make her look on me with interest?

INÉS [*aside to* Doña Leonor].
Oh Leonor! Don Rodrigo has good reason to come here; after all, I myself wrote him to come and get the ribbon.

LEONOR.
Fabia is responsible for this deception.

INÉS.
I'll tear up the note right away; I want to avenge myself on it for having slept in my bosom.

Enter Don Pedro, *her father, and* Don Fernando [*with the green ribbon on his hat*].

FERNANDO [*aside to* Don Pedro].
Don Rodrigo has appointed me his intermediary to arrange this matter with you.

PEDRO.
Well, then, the two of us will talk about the marriage agreement first.

FERNANDO.
But Rodrigo is already here; love is always a fast clock.

PEDRO.
Inés must have wound him up with the key of her favors.

FERNANDO.
He complains of just the opposite treatment.

PEDRO.	Señor don Rodrigo...	
RODRIGO.	Aquí	760
	vengo a que os sirváis de mí.	
INÉS.	Todo fue enredo de Fabia.	
LEONOR.	¿Cómo?	
INÉS.	¿No ves que también	
	trae el listón don Fernando?	
LEONOR.	Si en los dos le estoy mirando,	765
	entrambos te quieren bien.	
INÉS.	¡Sólo falta que me pidas	
	celos, cuando estoy sin mí!	
LEONOR.	¿Qué quieren tratar aquí?	
INÉS.	¿Ya las palabras olvidas	770
	que dijo mi padre ayer	
	en materia de casarme?	
LEONOR.	Luego bien puede olvidarme	
	Fernando, si él viene a ser.	
INÉS.	Antes presumo que son	775
	entrambos los que han querido	
	casarse, pues han partido	
	entre los dos el listón.	
PEDRO.	Esta es materia que quiere	
	secreto y espacio; entremos	780
	donde mejor la tratemos.	
RODRIGO.	Como yo ser vuestro espere,	
	no tengo más que tratar.	

PEDRO.

My lord Don Rodrigo—

RODRIGO.

Here I am, at your service.

[Don Pedro, Don Rodrigo, *and* Don Fernando *talk
together in a low voice.*]

INÉS [*aside to* Doña Leonor].

It was all a scheme of Fabia's.

LEONOR.

What do you mean?

INÉS.

Don't you see that Don Fernando is also wearing the ribbon?

LEONOR.

Since I see they're both wearing it, both of them must be in
love with you.

INÉS.

All I needed was for you to be jealous of me, just now when I'm
beside myself!

LEONOR.

What can they be talking about over there?

INÉS.

Have you already forgotten what father said yesterday about
marrying me off?

LEONOR.

In that case, Fernando can certainly forget me if he's to be the
groom.

INÉS.

On the contrary, I imagine they both want to get married, since
they've divided the ribbon between them.

PEDRO [*to* Don Rodrigo *and* Don Fernando].

This is a matter which demands privacy and time; let's go in the
other room where we can talk about it more freely.

RODRIGO.

As long as I may hope to be your son-in-law, I've nothing more
to discuss.

PEDRO.	Aunque os quiero enamorado	
	de Inés, para el nuevo estado,	785
	quien soy os ha de obligar.	*Vanse los tres.*
INÉS.	¡Qué vana fue mi esperanza!	
	¡Qué loco mi pensamiento!	
	¡Yo papel a don Rodrigo!	
	¡Y tú de Fernando celos!	790
	¡Oh forastero enemigo!	

Sale Fabia.

¡Oh Fabia embustera!

FABIA.   Quedo,
que lo está escuchando Fabia.
INÉS.   Pues ¿cómo, enemiga, has hecho
un enredo semejante?   795
FABIA. Antes fue tuyo el enredo,
si en aquel papel escribes
que fuese aquel caballero
por un listón de esperanza
a las rejas de tu güerto,   800
y en ellas pones dos hombres
que le maten, aunque pienso
que a no se haber retirado
pagaran su loco intento.
INÉS.   ¡Ay, Fabia! Ya que contigo   805
llego a declarar mi pecho,
ya que a mi padre, a mi estado
y a mi honor pierdo el respeto,
dime: ¿es verdad lo que dices?
Que siendo ansí, los que fueron   810
a la reja le tomaron
y por favor se le han puesto.
De suerte estoy, madre mía,
que no puedo hallar sosiego
si no es pensando en quien sabes.   815
FABIA. ¡Oh, qué bravo efeto hicieron
los hechizos y conjuros!
La vitoria me prometo.
No te desconsueles, hija;
vuelve en ti, que tendrás presto   820

PEDRO.

I'm glad you're in love with Inés, but I'm an honorable man and must make a proper agreement to bind you to this new state of matrimony.

Exeunt [Don Pedro, Don Rodrigo, *and* Don Fernando].

INÉS.

How vain were my hopes! How foolish my thoughts! To think that I should have sent a note to Don Rodrigo! And that you should be jealous of Fernando! Oh stranger, my enemy!

Enter Fabia.

Oh lying Fabia!

FABIA.

Softly, for Fabia is listening to it all.

INÉS.

Oh fiendish woman, how did you manage to tangle things up so?

FABIA.

I'm not responsible. This mess is all your fault if you wrote that young gentleman saying he should come to the garden grating to get the green ribbon of hope and then you put two men there to kill him. Even so, I think that if they hadn't run off, they would have paid dear for their foolish attempt.

INÉS.

Oh Fabia! Since I have come to the point of confessing my heart's longings to you, since I have lost respect for my father, my station, and my honor, tell me: Is what you say true? If that's the case, then Rodrigo and Fernando took the ribbon from the grating and are wearing it because they think it's a token of love. I am in such a state, good mother, that I can find no peace except in thoughts of the man you know.

FABIA [*aside*].

Oh how well my charms and spells have done their work! I promise myself the victory. —Don't give up hope, child; control yourself. Soon you'll be married to the best and noblest knight

estado con el mejor
y más noble caballero
que agora tiene Castilla;
porque será por lo menos
el que por único llaman   825
el caballero de Olmedo.
Don Alonso en una feria
te vio labradora Venus,
haciendo las cejas arco
y flecha los ojos bellos.   830
Disculpa tuvo en seguirte,
porque dicen los discretos
que consiste la hermosura
en ojos y entendimiento.
En fin, en las verdes cintas   835
de tus pies llevastes presos
los suyos, que ya el amor
no prende con los cabellos.
Él te sirve, tú le estimas;
él te adora, tú le has muerto;   840
él te escribe, tú respondes:
¿quién culpa amor tan honesto?
Para él tienen sus padres,
porque es único heredero,
diez mil ducados de renta;   845
y aunque es tan mozo, son viejos.
Déjate amar y servir
del más noble, del más cuerdo
caballero de Castilla,
lindo talle, lindo ingenio.   850
El Rey en Valladolid
grandes mercedes le ha hecho,
porque él solo honró las fiestas
de su real casamiento.
Cuchilladas y lanzadas   855
dio en los toros como un Héctor;
treinta precios dio a las damas
en sortijas y torneos.
Armado parece Aquiles
mirando de Troya el cerco;   860

in all Castile today, because your husband will be that man who stands so far above the rest that they call him the "Knight of Olmedo." At the fair Don Alonso saw you as Venus herself dressed like a peasant; your eyebrows served as Cupid's bow and your bright eyes as his arrows. He must be pardoned for following you, since wise men say that beauty resides in the eyes and in the intelligence. So you enchained his feet with the green ribbons on your own; after all, love no longer ensnares its victims in the lady's hair.[28] He serves you, you esteem him; he adores you, you have slain him; he writes to you, you answer him. Who can condemn so honorable a love? He's his parents' only heir, and they'll leave him an income of ten thousand ducats; and even though he's so young, they are old. Let yourself be loved and served by the noblest and most discreet knight in all Castile. A fine figure of a man, a fine mind. At the royal wedding festivities in Valladolid, the King[29] bestowed handsome gifts upon him because Don Alonso's feats in the chivalric games were enough by themselves to lend glory and honor to the occasion. He fought the bulls with his lance like Hector himself, and in the games[30] and tourneys he won thirty prizes, all of which he distributed to the ladies. Clad in armor he seems Achilles overseeing the siege of Troy; dressed in courtly

	con galas parece Adonis;	
	¡mejor fin le den los cielos!	
	Vivirás bien empleada	
	en un marido discreto.	
	¡Desdichada de la dama	865
	que tiene marido necio!	
INÉS.	¡Ay, madre! Vuélvesme loca.	
	Pero, ¡triste!, ¿cómo puedo	
	ser suya, si a don Rodrigo	
	me da mi padre don Pedro?	870
	Él y don Fernando están	
	tratando mi casamiento.	
FABIA.	Los dos harán nulidad	
	la sentencia de ese pleito.	
INÉS.	Está don Rodrigo allí.	875
FABIA.	Eso no te cause miedo,	
	pues es parte y no jüez.	
INÉS.	Leonor, ¿no me das consejo?	
LEONOR.	Y ¿estás tú para tomarle?	
INÉS.	No sé; pero no tratemos	880
	en público destas cosas.	
FABIA.	Déjame a mí tu suceso.	
	Don Alonso ha de ser tuyo;	
	que serás dichosa espero	
	con hombre que es en Castilla	885
	la gala de Medina,	
	la flor de Olmedo.	

Fin del primer acto del *Caballero de Olmedo*.

---

873. *harán*] 1641; *haréis* H.

finery he seems Adonis. May heaven grant him a better end![31]
You will be a fortunate wife with so discreet a husband.
Unhappy the woman who has a stupid mate!

INÉS.

Oh good mother, you'll drive me mad! But, alas, how can I be
his if my father Don Pedro betrothes me to Don Rodrigo? Right
now my father and Don Fernando are discussing my marriage.

FABIA.

The two of them will never come to any decision about that
suit.[32]

INÉS.

But Don Rodrigo is there now.

FABIA.

Don't worry about that. After all, he's one of the interested
parties and not the judge.

INÉS.

Leonor, won't you give me some advice?

LEONOR.

Are you in any mood to accept it?

INÉS.

I don't know. But let's not talk about these matters until we're
alone.

FABIA.

Leave everything to me. Don Alonso shall be yours. I expect
you're going to be happy with the man who is the glory of
Medina and the flower of Olmedo.

[*Exeunt.*]

End of the first act of *The Knight of Olmedo.*

ACTO SEGUNDO

Salen Tello y Don Alonso.

ALONSO.   Tengo el morir por mejor,
          Tello, que vivir sin ver.
TELLO.   Temo que se ha de saber   890
          este tu secreto amor;
              que con tanto ir y venir
          de Olmedo a Medina, creo
          que a los dos da tu deseo
          que sentir y aun que decir.   895
ALONSO.   ¿Cómo puedo yo dejar
          de ver a Inés, si la adoro?
TELLO.   Guardándole más decoro
          en el venir y el hablar;
              que en ser a tercero día,   900
          pienso que te dan, señor,
          tercianas de amor.
ALONSO.   Mi amor
          ni está ocioso, ni se enfría;
              siempre abrasa, y no permite
          que esfuerce naturaleza   905
          un instante su flaqueza,
          porque jamás se remite.
              Mas bien se ve que es león
          amor; su fuerza, tirana;
          pues que con esta cuartana   910
          se amansa mi corazón.
              Es esta ausencia una calma
          de amor; porque si estuviera
          adonde siempre a Inés viera,
          fuera salamandra el alma.   915
TELLO.   ¿No te cansa y te amohína
          tanto entrar, tanto partir?

---

909. *su fuerza, tirana*] 1641; *tu fuerza tirana* H.

ACT II

[The street in front of Don Pedro's house.]
Enter Tello *and* Don Alonso.

ALONSO.

I think death is better, Tello, than life without seeing her.

TELLO.

I'm afraid people are going to find out about your secret love affair. So much going back and forth between Olmedo and Medina is bound to make both towns notice your love and gossip about it.

ALONSO.

How can I stop seeing Inés when I adore her?

TELLO.

You should at least be more careful about her reputation when you come to see her and talk to her. But you come every third day, which makes me think you're suffering from a tertian fever of love!

ALONSO.

My love is not idle, nor does it grow cold: it is always aflame and has no need for nature to fan its weakness even an instant, because it never dies down. But truly love is a lion and tyrannical in its force, although on the fourth day, when I'm away from Inés, my heart's fever is soothed. This separation is a calm on the sea of love; if I were where I might see her always, my soul would be a salamander.³³

TELLO.

Doesn't so much coming and going wear you out and vex you?

ALONSO. Pues yo ¿qué hago en venir,
Tello, de Olmedo a Medina?
  Leandro pasaba un mar   920
todas las noches, por ver
si le podía beber
para poderse templar.
  Pues si entre Olmedo y Medina
no hay, Tello, un mar, ¿qué me debe   925
Inés?

TELLO.   A otro mar se atreve
quien al peligro camina
  en que Leandro se vio;
pues a don Rodrigo veo
tan cierto de tu deseo   930
como puedo estarlo yo;
  que como yo no sabía
cúya aquella capa fue,
un día que la saqué...

ALONSO. ¡Gran necedad!

TELLO.   como mía,   935
  me preguntó: «Diga, hidalgo,
¿quién esta capa le dio?
Porque la conozco yo.»
Respondí: «Si os sirve en algo,
daréla a un criado vuestro.»   940
  Con esto, descolorido,
dijo: «Habíala perdido
de noche un lacayo nuestro;
pero mejor empleada
está en vos: guardadla bien.»   945
  Y fuese a medio desdén,
puesta la mano en la espada.
  Sabe que te sirvo y sabe
que la perdió con los dos.
Advierte, señor, por Dios,   950
que toda esta gente es grave,
  y que están en su lugar,
donde todo gallo canta.
  Sin esto, también me espanta
ver este amor comenzar   955

ALONSO.

It's a small thing, Tello, to go back and forth between Olmedo and Medina. Leander crossed a sea every night to see whether, by drinking it, he might temper his love's flame. Well, since there's no sea, Tello, between Olmedo and Medina, what sacrifice do I make for Inés?

TELLO.

He who sets out on the same dangerous course as Leander dares another kind of sea. Don Rodrigo, I think, is as certain of your love as I myself am, because, since I didn't know whose cape that was, one day when I put it on—

ALONSO.

A stupid mistake!

TELLO.

—as if it were mine, he asked me: "Tell me, my friend, who gave you that cape, because I recognize it?" I answered, "If it's of any use to you, I'll give it to one of your servants." He turned pale and said, "A lackey of ours lost it one night, but it looks better on you; take good care of it." And he went off pretending he wasn't interested but with his hand on his sword. He knows I'm your servant and that he lost it fighting with the two of us. Don't forget, master, for God's sake, that these people here are touchy and proud and that they're on their home ground, where every rooster thinks he's the cock of the walk. But leaving all that aside, it also frightens me to see this

         por tantas hechicerías,
         y que cercos y conjuros
         no son remedios seguros,
         si honestamente porfías.
             Fui con ella ¡que no fuera!   960
         a sacar de un ahorcado
         una muela; puse a un lado,
         como Arlequín, la escalera.
             Subió Fabia, quedé al pie,
         y díjome el salteador: 965
         «Sube, Tello, sin temor,
         o si no, yo bajaré.»
             ¡San Pablo, allí me caí!
         Tan sin alma vine al suelo,
         que fue milagro del cielo   970
         el poder volver en mí.
             Bajó, desperté turbado,
         y de mirarme afligido,
         porque, sin haber llovido,
         estaba todo mojado.   975
ALONSO.   Tello, un verdadero amor
         en ningún peligro advierte.
             Quiso mi contraria suerte
         que hubiese competidor,
         y que trate, enamorado,   980
         casarse con doña Inés;
         pues ¿qué he de hacer, si me ves
         celoso y desesperado?
             No creo en hechicerías,
         que todas son vanidades;   985
         quien concierta voluntades,
         son méritos y porfías.
             Inés me quiere, yo adoro
         a Inés, yo vivo en Inés;
         todo lo que Inés no es   990
         desprecio, aborrezco, ignoro.
             Inés es mi bien, yo soy
         esclavo de Inés; no puedo

love affair start off with so much witchcraft; magical circles and spells are not safe means if your suit is honorable. I went with Fabia—heaven knows I wish I hadn't—to extract a tooth from a hanged man; like Harlequin, I set the ladder against the side of the gallows.[34] Fabia climbed up; I stayed at the foot, and the highwayman suddenly spoke to me: "Come on up, Tello, don't be afraid; or if you don't, I'll come down." Holy Saint Paul! Right there I fell to the ground in a dead faint;[35] it was a miracle from heaven that I ever came to my senses. Fabia came down; I woke up all confused, and grieved to see the shape I was in, because, even though it hadn't rained, I was wet clear through.[36]

ALONSO.

Tello, true love takes no notice of danger. The hostile stars willed that I should have a rival for Inés's love who was trying to marry her. Well, then, what am I to do, if I'm both jealous and despairing? I don't believe in witchcraft; it's idle and vain. What brings two people's wills into harmony is one's own worth and unfailing love. Inés loves me, I adore Inés, I live in Inés; all that is not Inés I scorn, abhor, and cannot see. Inés is all my treasure, I am her slave; I cannot live without Inés; I go back

	vivir sin Inés; de Olmedo	
	a Medina vengo y voy,	995
	porque Inés mi dueño es	
	para vivir o morir.	
TELLO.	Sólo te falta decir:	
	«Un poco te quiero, Inés.»	
	¡Plega a Dios que por bien sea!	1000
ALONSO.	Llama, que es hora.	
TELLO.	Yo voy.	
ANA.	¿Quién es?	
TELLO.	¡Tan presto! Yo soy.	
	¿Está en casa Melibea?	
	Que viene Calisto aquí.	
ANA.	Aguarda un poco, Sempronio.	1005
TELLO.	Sí haré, falso testimonio.	

Sale Doña Inés.

INÉS.	¿El mismo?	
ANA.	Señora, sí.	
INÉS.	¡Señor mío!	
ALONSO.	Bella Inés,	
	esto es venir a vivir.	
TELLO.	Agora no hay que decir:	1010
	«Yo te lo diré después.»	
INES.	¡Tello amigo!	
TELLO.	¡Reina mía!	

1003-1007. *¿Está* ... *sí*] 1641, H; R punctuates vs. 1006 as "*¿Si haré falso testimonio?*" The line thus means, "Would I be telling a lie?" (Neither solution is totally satisfactory, though R's reading would be most appropriate if the lines were rearranged [and perhaps they should be] as follows: Tello. ¿Está en casa Melibea?/ Ana. Aguarda un poco, Sempronio./ Tello. Que viene Calisto aquí./Inés. ¿El mismo? Tello. Señora, sí./¿Si haré falso testimonio?) H puts Inés's entrance after vs. 1007.

and forth between Olmedo and Medina because Inés is my mistress in life and in death.

TELLO.

Well, there's very little to be added to that speech except "Inés, I love you a little anyway."³⁷ May it please God that everything turns out well.

ALONSO.

Knock on the door. It's time now.

TELLO.

I'm going.   *[Knocks at the door of Don Pedro's house.]*

ANA [*off*].

Who is it?

TELLO.

So quickly! It's me. Is Melibea at home? Calisto's here to see her.

ANA [*off*].

Wait a minute, Sempronio.

TELLO.

So I will, you liar.³⁸

[Ana *opens the door, and* Don Alonso *and* Tello *enter a room in Don Pedro's house.*]
Enter Doña Inés.

INÉS [*to* Ana].

Is it he?

ANA.

Yes, mistress.

INÉS.

My lord!

ALONSO.

Lovely Inés, seeing you is to live fully.

TELLO.

Now there's no need to say, "I'll tell you I love you some day."³⁹

INÉS.

Tello, my friend!

TELLO.

My queen!

INÉS.   Nunca, Alonso de mis ojos,
            por haberme dado enojos
            esta ignorante porfía   1015
            de don Rodrigo esta tarde,
            he estimado que me vieses.
ALONSO.   Aunque fuerza de obediencia
            te hiciese tomar estado,
            no he de estar desengañado   1020
            hasta escuchar la sentencia.
            Bien el alma me decía,
            y a Tello se lo contaba
            cuando el caballo sacaba
            y el sol los que aguarda el día,   1025
            que de alguna novedad
            procedía mi tristeza,
            viniendo a ver tu belleza,
            pues me dices que es verdad.
            ¡Ay de mí si ha sido ansí!   1030
INÉS.   No lo creas, porque yo
            diré a todo el mundo no,
            después que te dije sí.
            Tú solo dueño has de ser
            de mi libertad y vida;   1035
            no hay fuerza que el ser impida,
            don Alonso, tu mujer.
            Bajaba al jardín ayer,
            y como por don Fernando
            me voy de Leonor guardando,   1040
            a las fuentes, a las flores
            estuve diciendo amores,
            y estuve también llorando.
            «Flores y aguas, les decía,
            dichosa vida gozáis,   1045
            pues aunque noche pasáis,
            veis vuestro sol cada día.»
            Pensé que me respondía
            la lengua de una azucena

1017-1018. *he ... obediencia*] 1641; at least two lines are missing from the text
here, for the *redondilla* begun in vs. 1016 lacks two lines to complete the normal *a b b a*
rhyme scheme.

INÉS.

Dearest Alonso, after the trouble Don Rodrigo gave me with his senseless courtship this afternoon, I didn't let myself hope you would ever see me.

ALONSO.

Even though filial obedience should force you to accept marriage to him,[40] I refuse to lose hope until I've heard my sentence from you. My heart warned me of unhappiness. I told Tello when be brought my horse, at the hour when Phoebus brings out his steeds and day breaks,[41] that some new turn of events must have inspired my melancholy just as I was setting out to gaze upon your loveliness; and now you tell me I was right in my fears. How wretched I am if you have accepted his suit!

INÉS.

Never believe such a thing, for I'll say no to all the world once I've said yes to you. You alone shall be the master of my life and liberty; there is no power on earth which can prevent my being your wife. Yesterday I went down into the garden, and since I keep away from Leonor because she loves Fernando, I told the story of my love to the fountains and the flowers, and I also wept. "Fountains and flowers," I said to them, "Your life is fortunate, for even though you must endure the night, you see your sun each day." And I fancied that a lily's tongue

          ¡qué engaños amor ordena!:   1050
          «Si el sol que adorando estás
          viene de noche, que es más,
          Inés, ¿de qué tienes pena?»

TELLO.   Así dijo a un ciego un griego
          que le contó mil disgustos: 1055
          «Pues tiene la noche gustos,
          ¿para qué te quejas, ciego?»

INÉS.   Como mariposa llego
          a estas horas, deseosa
          de tu luz. No mariposa,   1060
          fénix ya, pues de una suerte
          me da vida y me da muerte
          llama tan dulce y hermosa.

ALONSO.   ¡Bien haya el coral, amén,
          de cuyas hojas de rosas   1065
          palabras tan amorosas
          salen a buscar mi bien!
          Y advierte que yo también,
          cuando con Tello no puedo,
          mis celos, mi amor, mi miedo   1070
          digo en tu ausencia a las flores.

TELLO.   Yo le vi decir amores
          a los rábanos de Olmedo;
          que un amante suele hablar
          con las piedras, con el viento.   1075

ALONSO.   No puede mi pensamiento
          ni estar solo, ni callar;
          contigo, Inés, ha de estar,
          contigo hablar y sentir.
          ¡Oh, quién supiera decir   1080
          lo que te digo en ausencia!
          Pero estando en tu presencia
          aun se me olvida el vivir.
          Por el camino le cuento
          tus gracias a Tello, Inés,   1085
          y celebramos después
          tu divino entendimiento.

1078. *contigo*] H; *contiguo* 1641.

replied (how love deceives us!): "If the sun you worship, Inés, comes by night, which is a more splendid blessing, why are you sad?"

TELLO.

For that same reason a certain Greek said to a blind man who had told him his infinite misfortunes: "Since the night holds so many pleasures, why do you complain because you can't see?"

INÉS.

I come to these hours like a butterfly, eager for your light. But no, that's not it. Not like a butterfly, but like the phoenix, for the sweet and beautiful flame of your love gives me life and gives me death both at the same time.[42]

ALONSO.

Heaven bless your coral mouth and the rose petals of your lips from which fall those words that bring me bliss. I too, when you are absent and I cannot speak with Tello, recount my jealousy, my love, my fear to the flowers.

TELLO.

I've even seen him talking about his love to the radishes in Olmedo. A lover is wont to talk with stones or to the wind.

ALONSO.

My thoughts cannot endure either solitude or silence; they must be with you, Inés, they must speak and feel with you. Oh, would that I could repeat what I say to you in your absence! But when I'm in your presence, I forget my very life. On the road I tell Tello all the witty and charming things you've said, and we celebrate your heavenly intelligence. I sense such glory

            Tal gloria en tu nombre siento,
            que una mujer recibí
            de tu nombre, porque ansí,   1090
            llamándola todo el día,
            pienso, Inés, señora mía,
            que te estoy llamando a ti.
TELLO.   Pues advierte, Inés discreta,
            de los dos tan nuevo efeto,   1095
            que a él le has hecho discreto,
            y a mí me has hecho poeta.
            Oye una glosa a un estribo
            que compuso don Alonso,
            a manera de responso,   1100
            si los hay en muerto vivo.
                En el valle a Inés
                la dejé riendo.
                Si la ves, Andrés,
                dile cuál me ves   1105
                por ella muriendo.
INÉS.   ¿Don Alonso la compuso?
TELLO.   Que es buena jurarte puedo
            para poeta de Olmedo.
            Escucha.
ALONSO.   Amor lo dispuso.   1110
TELLO.   Andrés, después que las bellas
            plantas de Inés goza el valle,
            tanto florece con ellas,
            que quiso el cielo trocalle
            por sus flores sus estrellas.   1115
            Ya el valle es cielo, después
            que su primavera es,
            pues verá el cielo en el suelo
            quien vio, pues Inés es cielo,
            en el valle a Inés.   1120

    1119. *quien ... cielo*] M; *quien vio pues Inés el cielo* 1641; *Quien vio, pues de Inés es cielo* H.

in your name that I've employed a serving girl who bears it so that when I summon her the whole day long, I fancy, oh my fair Inés, that I am calling you.

TELLO.

Just see, oh discreet Inés, the new and wonderful change you've wrought in both of us: you've made him discreet and me you've turned into a poet. Listen to the verses I've written around a stanza Don Alonso composed in the form of a prayer for the dead—if there are such things for the living dead.

I last saw Inés
laughing in the valley;
if you see her, Andrés,
tell her how you found me,
dying for her love.

INÉS.

Don Alonso composed those lines?[4][3]

TELLO.

And I can testify that it's a good piece for a poet from Olmedo. Listen to it.

ALONSO.

Love arranged the words.

TELLO.

So long, Andrés, as the vale's enjoyed
Inés's fair and dancing feet,
it's bloomed so richly under them
that heaven's sought to make a trade:
its glowing stars for valley flowers.
And now the vale itself is heaven
because Inés has brought its spring;
and he will see a heaven on earth
who sees her there, for she is heaven, as
I last saw Inés.

Con miedo y respeto estampo
el pie donde el suyo huella;
que ya Medina del Campo
no quiere aurora más bella
para florecer su campo.　　　　　　　1125
Yo la vi de amor huyendo,
cuanto miraba matando,
su mismo desdén venciendo;
y aunque me partí llorando,
la dejé riendo.　　　　　　　1130

Dile, Andrés, que ya me veo
muerto por volverla a ver,
aunque, cuando llegues, creo
que no será menester,
que me habrá muerto el deseo.　　　　1135
No tendrás que hacer después
que a sus manos vengativas
llegues, si una vez la ves,
ni aun es posible que vivas,
si la ves, Andrés.　　　　　　　1140

Pero si matarte olvida
por no hacer caso de ti,
dile a mi hermosa homicida
que por qué se mata en mí,
pues que sabe que es mi vida.　　　　1145
Dile: «Cruel, no le des
muerte, si vengada estás
y te ha de pesar después.»
Y pues no me has de ver más,
dile cuál me ves.　　　　　　　1150

1150. me ves] H; *le ves* 1641.

With fear and reverence I plant
my foot where hers has often stepped;
for now Medina's countryside
desires no dawn more bright and gold
to bring its fields to richest flower.
I saw her there in flight from love
and slaying all she gazed upon
despite her constant cruel scorn,
and as I parted, weeping, I left her
      laughing in the valley.

Tell her, Andrés, I pine and die
of longing hope to see my love,
though if by chance you meet her once
I think the words will be in vain,
for I shall then be dead from pain.
Your words will die upon the wind
when you come near her vengeful hand;
if once you chance to see her face,
you too have lost all hope of life,
      if you see her, Andrés.

But if she fails to end your life,
because she will not raise her eyes,
then ask my lovely murderess
no more than this: "Why slay herself
in me, knowing she is all my life?"
And add, "Oh cruel lady, slay him not,
for you're already well avenged,
and one day you will feel regret."
And since again we shall not meet,
      tell her how you found me.

Verdad es que se dilata
el morir, pues con mirar
vuelve a dar vida la ingrata,
y así se cansa en matar,
pues da vida a cuantos mata.   1155
Pero muriendo o viviendo,
no me pienso arrepentir
de estarla amando y sirviendo;
que no hay bien como vivir
por ella muriendo.   1160

INÉS.   Si es tuya, notablemente
te has alargado en mentir
por don Alonso.

ALONSO.   Es decir,
que mi amor en versos miente.
Pues, señora, ¿qué poesía   1165
llegará a significar
mi amor?

INÉS.   ¡Mi padre!

ALONSO.   ¿Ha de entrar?

INÉS.   Escondeos.

ALONSO.   ¿Dónde?

Ellos se entran, y sale Don Pedro.

PEDRO.   Inés mía,
¿agora por recoger?
¿Como no te has acostado?   1170

INÉS.   Rezando, señor, he estado,
por lo que dijiste ayer,
rogando a Dios que me incline
a lo que fuere mejor.

PEDRO.   Cuando para ti mi amor   1175
imposibles imagine,
no pudiera hallar un hombre
como don Rodrigo, Inés.

> It's true that death delays its sting,
> for every glance my lady grants
> stirs life once more within my soul;
> and she tires thus of slaying men,
> for she gives life to all she kills.
> But be it living or be it dying,
> my heart will never falter once
> in loving her and serving her,
> for there's no good so great as living,
> *dying for her love.*

INÉS.

If that's really your poem, Tello, you've certainly spent a lot of words on lying in your master's cause.

ALONSO.

In other words, you think my love tells lies in verse. But, my lady, what poetry could possibly express the depth and meaning of my love?

INÉS.

My father's coming!

ALONSO.

Will he come in here?

INÉS.

Both of you hide.

ALONSO.

Where?

They go out, and Don Pedro *enters.*

PEDRO.

But Inés, you're still up! Why haven't you gone to bed?

INÉS.

I've been praying, sir, about what you said yesterday,[44] begging God to turn my will into the best path.

PEDRO.

Inés, if my love for you had sought the impossible in the way of a husband, I couldn't have found a man better than Don Rodrigo.

INÉS. Ansí dicen todos que es
de su buena fama el nombre;   1180
y habiéndome de casar,
ninguno en Medina hubiera,
ni en Castilla, que pudiera
sus méritos igualar.
PEDRO. ¿Cómo, habiendo de casarte?   1185
INÉS. Señor, hasta ser forzoso
decir que ya tengo esposo,
no he querido disgustarte.
PEDRO. ¡Esposo! ¿Qué novedad
es ésta, Inés?
INÉS.   Para ti   1190
será novedad, que en mí
siempre fue mi voluntad.
Y, ya que estoy declarada,
hazme mañana cortar
un hábito, para dar   1195
fin a esta gala escusada;
que así quiero andar, señor,
mientras me enseñan latín.
Leonor te queda, que al fin
te dará nietos Leonor.   1200
Y por mi madre te ruego
que en esto no me repliques,
sino que medios apliques
a mi elección y sosiego.
Haz buscar una mujer   1205
de buena y santa opinión,
que me dé alguna lición
de lo que tengo de ser,
y un maestro de cantar,
que de latín sea también.   1210
PEDRO. ¿Eres tú quien habla, o quién?
INÉS. Esto es hacer, no es hablar.
PEDRO. Por una parte, mi pecho
se enternece de escucharte,
Inés, y por otra parte,   1215
de duro mármol le has hecho.

INÉS.

That's what everybody says about his fine reputation, and if I were to marry, there wouldn't be anyone in Medina or even in all Castile to equal his merits.

PEDRO.

What do you mean, "if I were to marry"?

INÉS.

Until it was necessary, sir, I hadn't wanted to displease you by saying that I already have a husband.[45]

PEDRO.

You already have a husband! What new idea is this you're talking about, Inés?

INÉS.

For you it may be something new, but it has always been my will. And now that I've confessed it, tomorrow have them make me a nun's habit so that I can get rid of this unnecessary finery. I wish to dress that way, sir, while they are teaching me Latin. You've still got Leonor, and she will give you grandchildren. For my mother's sake I beg you not to oppose me in this but to help me in the choice I've made for the peace of my soul. Find me a woman of good and saintly reputation who can give me some lessons about my future life as a nun, and also a singing master who can instruct me in Latin too.

PEDRO.

Is it really you who are talking or someone else?

INÉS.

These are actions, not idle words.

PEDRO.

In one sense my heart grows tender as I listen to you, Inés, but in another, you've frozen it as hard as marble. In my declining

En tu verde edad mi vida
esperaba sucesión;
pero si esto es vocación,
no quiera Dios que lo impida.   1220
   Haz tu gusto, aunque tu celo
en esto no intenta el mío;
que ya sé que el albedrío
no presta obediencia al cielo.
   Pero porque suele ser   1225
nuestro pensamiento humano
tal vez inconstante y vano,
y en condición de mujer,
   que es fácil de persuadir,
tan poca firmeza alcanza,   1230
que hay de mujer a mudanza
lo que de hacer a decir,
   mudar las galas no es justo,
pues no pueden estorbar
a leer latín o cantar,   1235
ni a cuanto fuere tu gusto.
   Viste alegre y cortesana,
que no quiero que Medina,
si hoy te admirare divina,
mañana te burle humana.   1240
   Yo haré buscar la mujer
y quien te enseñe latín,
pues a mejor padre, en fin,
es más justo obedecer.
   Y con esto, a Dios te queda;   1245
que, para no darte enojos,
van a esconderse mis ojos
adonde llorarte pueda.

Vase, y salgan Don Alonso *y* Tello.

INÉS.   Pésame de haberte dado
disgusto.

years I had hoped for heirs from your fresh youth; but if this is your true vocation, God forbid that I should stand in your way. Do as you will, even though your piety in this matter goes against my wishes; after all, I know that one's own willful desires do not always obey heaven's intentions. But human thoughts are sometimes inconstant and fickle, and they show so little firmness in women, who are easily swayed, that what a woman says and what she does are two different things. So there's no reason to change your style of dress, for fine clothes can't keep you from reading Latin or singing or whatever you want to do. Dress with elegance and gaiety; I wouldn't want Medina to revere you one day as a saint and make fun of you the next as all too human. I'll look for the devout woman you want and someone to teach you Latin, for it is meet and proper to obey the Heavenly Father rather than the earthly one. And now I'll say no more. God keep you. I shall retire where my tears will not distress you.

He goes out, and Don Alonso *and* Tello *enter.*

INÉS.
I'm sorry, my lord, to have inconvenienced you this way.

ALONSO.	A mí no me pesa,	1250
	por el que me ha dado el ver	
	que nuestra muerte conciertas.	
	¡Ay, Inés! ¿Adónde hallaste	
	en tal desdicha, en tal pena,	
	tan breve remedio?	
INÉS.	Amor	1255
	en los peligros enseña	
	una luz por donde el alma	
	posibles remedios vea.	
ALONSO.	Este ¿es remedio posible?	
INÉS.	Como yo agora le tenga	1260
	para que este don Rodrigo	
	no llegue al fin que desea,	
	bien sabes que breves males	
	la dilación los remedia;	
	que no dejan esperanza	1265
	si no hay segunda sentencia.	
TELLO.	Dice bien, señor; que en tanto	
	que doña Inés cante y lea,	
	podéis dar orden los dos	
	para que os valga la Iglesia.	1270
	Sin esto, desconfiado	
	don Rodrigo, no hará fuerza	
	a don Pedro en la palabra,	
	pues no tendrá por ofensa	
	que le deje doña Inés	1275
	por quien dice que le deja.	
	También es linda ocasión	
	para que yo vaya y venga	
	con libertad a esta casa.	
ALONSO.	¡Libertad! ¿De qué manera?	1280
TELLO.	Pues ha de leer latín,	
	¿no será fácil que pueda	
	ser yo quien venga a enseñarla?	
	¡Y verás con qué destreza	
	la enseño a leer tus cartas!	1285

1252. *conciertas*] H; *concierta* 1641.
1257. *por donde*] H; *donde* 1641; *adonde* M.

ALONSO.

Hiding's nothing at all in comparison with what I've just seen and heard: you've arranged it so we both shall die! Oh Inés, in such unhappiness and pain, how did you find a remedy so quickly?

INÉS.

In danger love shows one a light by means of which the soul glimpses possible remedies.

ALONSO.

But can this be a remedy?

INÉS.

It is, because now I've found a way to keep Don Rodrigo from achieving his purpose. You know that evils of short duration are remedied by delay, but there's no hope if there's not time for a second verdict.

TELLO.

She's right, master. While Doña Inés is singing and reading Latin, you two can arrange for the Church to come to your aid. Besides that, Don Rodrigo can't be sure of his ground and won't force Don Pedro to keep his word about the marriage, since he won't be offended if Inés abandons him for the bridegroom she alleges. It's also a fine opportunity for me to go and come freely in this house.

ALONSO.

Freely! How?

TELLO.

Since she's going to read Latin, won't it be easy to arrange for me to be the one who comes to teach her? Just wait and see how skillfully I teach her to read your letters!

ALONSO. ¡Que bien mi remedio piensas!

TELLO. Y aun pienso que podrá Fabia
servirte en forma de dueña,
siendo la santa mujer
que con su falsa apariencia   1290
venga a enseñarla.

INÉS.   Bien dices,
Fabia será mi maestra
de virtudes y costumbres.

TELLO. ¡Y qué tales serán ellas!

ALONSO. Mi bien, yo temo que el día,   1295
que es amor dulce materia
para no sentir las horas,
que por los amantes vuelan,
nos halle tan descuidados,
que al salir de aquí me vean,   1300
o que sea fuerza quedarme.
¡Ay, Dios! ¡Qué dichosa fuerza!
Medina a la Cruz de Mayo
hace sus mayores fiestas;
yo tengo que prevenir,   1305
que, como sabes, se acercan,
que, fuera de que en la plaza
quiero que galán me veas,
de Valladolid me escriben
que el rey don Juan viene a verlas;   1310
que en los montes de Toledo
le pide que se entretenga
el Condestable estos días,
porque en ellos convalezca,
y de camino, señora,   1315
que honre esta villa le ruega;
y así, es razón que le sirva
la nobleza desta tierra.
Guárdete el cielo, mi bien.

INÉS. Espera, que a abrir la puerta   1320
es forzoso que yo vaya.

ALONSO. ¡Ay, luz! ¡Ay, aurora necia,
de todo amante envidiosa!

TELLO. Ya no aguardéis que amanezca.

ALONSO. ¿Cómo?

ALONSO.

How cleverly you've thought up a way to save me!

TELLO.

And I'm also thinking that Fabia might serve you as a duenna. With her false air of piety she could be the saintly woman who comes to teach Inés.

INÉS.

You're right. Fabia will be my teacher of virtue and devout habits.

TELLO.

And you can bet what those devout habits will be like!

ALONSO.

My dearest, love's conversation is so sweet that lovers do not sense the flying hours; and I fear the dawn will find us unprepared, and that people will either see me when I leave or I'll be forced to stay here. Oh heavens, what a happy forced imprisonment that would be! You know that Medina celebrates its greatest festival on the Feast of the Finding of the Holy Cross,[46] which is coming soon now in May. I must make ready for it, because I want you to see me at my best in the bullfight, and besides I've heard from Valladolid that the King, Don Juan, is coming to see the festivities. On the advice of the Lord High Constable Don Alvaro de Luna[47] he's going to hunt in the woods around Toledo so that he may recover his strength; and on his way there the Constable has asked him to honor Medina with his presence. So it is only right that the nobles of this land should serve him in the festival games. May heaven keep you, my dearest.

INÉS.

Wait, for I must open the door for you.

ALONSO.

Oh vexing light of day! Oh foolish dawn, envious of all lovers!

TELLO.

Don't bother to wait now for dawn.

ALONSO.

Why?

TELLO.	Porque es de día.	1325
ALONSO.	Bien dices, si a Inés me muestras.	

Pero ¿cómo puede ser,
Tello, cuando el sol se acuesta?

TELLO.　Tú vas de espacio, él aprisa;
apostaré que te quedas.　　　　　　　　　1330

Salen Don Rodrigo *y* Don Fernando.

RODRIGO.　Muchas veces había reparado,
don Fernando, en aqueste caballero,
del corazón solícito avisado.
El talle, el grave rostro, lo severo,
celoso me obligaban a miralle.　　　　　　1335

FERNANDO.　Efetos son de amante verdadero,
que en viendo otra persona de buen talle,
tienen temor que si le ve su dama
será posible o fuerza codicialle.

RODRIGO.　Bien es verdad que él tiene tanta fama,　1340
que, por más que en Medina se encubría,
el mismo aplauso popular le aclama.
Vi, como os dije, aquel mancebo un día
que la capa perdida en la pendencia
contra el valor de mi opinión traía.　　　　1345
Hice secretamente diligencia,
después de hablarle, y satisfecho quedo,
que tiene esta amistad correspondencia.
Su dueño es don Alonso, aquel de Olmedo,
alanceador galán y cortesano,　　　　　　1350
de quien hombres y toros tienen miedo.
Pues si éste sirve a Inés, ¿qué intento en vano
o ¿cómo quiero yo, si ya le adora,
que Inés me mire con semblante humano?

FERNANDO.　¿Por fuerza ha de quererle?

RODRIGO.　　　　　　　　　　Él la enamora,　1355
y merece, Fernando, que le quiera.
¿Qué he de pensar, si me aborrece agora?

1330. *quedas*] 1641; the scene changes here, but 1641 does not indicate an exit; H does.

TELLO.

Because it's already full daylight.

ALONSO.

You're surely right if you're pointing to Inés. But how can it be day when the sun itself retires to bed with her?

TELLO.

You move slowly; the sun goes fast. I'll bet you stay behind here after all.   [*Exeunt.*]

[*A street in Medina.*]
Enter Don Rodrigo *and* Don Fernando.

RODRIGO.

Many times now, Don Fernando, put on guard by my diligent heart, I've noticed that fellow. His figure, his grave face, the severity of his bearing have forced me to look on him with jealous eyes.

FERNANDO.

That's normal behavior for men who are truly in love. Whenever they see another fellow who's good-looking, they're afraid that if their mistress sees him, she may, or even must, fall in love with him.

RODRIGO.

Besides that, he's so well known that even though he's kept under cover in Medina, the people sing his praises. As I told you, I saw that boy one day when he was wearing the cape we lost in the fight. His flaunting the cape that way is an affront to my good name. After I spoke to the boy, I secretly made inquiries about him and found out who his master is. I'm certain, furthermore, that his master's suit to Inés is favorably received by her, for the boy's master is none other than Don Alonso of Olmedo. He's a gallant and courtly swordsman, feared alike by men and bulls. If he's paying court to Inés, why do I bother to push my vain suit? If she already adores him, how can I expect Inés to look on me compassionately?

FERNANDO.

You think she's bound to be in love with him?

RODRIGO.

He's making love to her, Fernando, and he deserves to have his love returned. What else can I think when I see she despises me now?

FERNANDO.   Son celos, don Rodrigo, una quimera
que se forma de envidia, viento y sombra,
con que lo incierto, imaginado altera;   1360
una fantasma que de noche asombra,
un pensamiento que a locura inclina,
y una mentira que verdad se nombra.
RODRIGO.   Pues ¿cómo tantas veces a Medina
viene y va don Alonso? Y ¿a qué efeto   1365
es cédula de noche en una esquina?
Yo me quiero casar; vos sois discreto:
¿qué consejo me dais, si no es matalle?
FERNANDO.   Yo hago diferente mi conceto;
que ¿cómo puede doña Inés amalle,   1370
si nunca os quiso a vos?
RODRIGO.   Porque es respuesta
que tiene mayor dicha o mejor talle.
FERNANDO.   Mas porque doña Inés es tan honesta,
que aun la ofendéis con nombre de marido.
RODRIGO.   Yo he de matar a quien vivir me cuesta   1375
en su desgracia, porque tanto olvido
no puede proceder de honesto intento.
Perdí la capa y perderé el sentido.
FERNANDO.   Antes dejarla a don Alonso siento
que ha sido como echársela en los ojos.   1380
Ejecutad, Rodrigo, el casamiento;
llévese don Alonso los despojos,
y la vitoria vos.
RODRIGO.   Mortal desmayo
cubre mi amor de celos y de enojos.
FERNANDO.   Salid galán para la Cruz de Mayo,   1385
que yo saldré con vos; pues el Rey viene,
las sillas piden el castaño y bayo.
Menos aflige el mal que se entretiene.
RODRIGO.   Si viene don Alonso, ya Medina
¿qué competencia con Olmedo tiene?   1390

1373. *Mas . . . honesta*] H; *Mas porque es doña Inés tan honesta* 1641. The 1641
reading requires a rather unnatural syllabic division between *porque* and *es.*

FERNANDO.

You're only suffering from jealousy, Don Rodrigo, and jealousy is a chimera formed of envy, air, and shadows so that the imagination builds on the unknown to produce alarm; it's a ghost to startle one by night, a thought that drives one to madness, and a lie which calls itself the truth.

RODRIGO.

Then why does Don Alonso go back and forth so often between Medina and Olmedo? And why at night should he stand by the same wall as if he were stuck to it?[48] I want to marry Inés. You're an intelligent man. What advice can you give me if it's not to kill him?

FERNANDO.

I don't see things that way at all. Tell me, why should you think Inés loves him when she never showed the slightest love for you?

RODRIGO.

Simply because he's luckier or better-looking.

FERNANDO.

Maybe she treats you coldly because you offend her maidenly modesty by even mentioning marriage?

RODRIGO.

I swear I'll kill the man who makes me suffer her disfavor; such indifference to me can't spring from chaste intentions. Just as I lost my cape, I'll lose my mind.

FERNANDO.

I think, rather, that letting the cape fall into Don Alonso's hands was a way of fooling him and favoring yourself.[49] Rodrigo, go ahead and get married. Let Don Alonso carry off the spoils as long as you win the victory.

RODRIGO.

I feel a deadly weakness that shadows my love with jealousy and pain.

FERNANDO.

Take heart. Make a gallant showing at the festival of the Cross. I'll accompany you. The King is coming, and the chestnut and the bay demand their saddles. A bit of diversion eases any pain.

RODRIGO.

If Don Alonso takes part, how can Medina compete with Olmedo?

FERNANDO. ¡Qué loco estáis!

RODRIGO. Amor me desatina. *Vanse.*

Salen Don Pedro, Doña Inés, Doña Leonor.

PEDRO. No porfíes.

INÉS. No podrás
mi propósito vencer.

PEDRO. Hija, ¿qué quieres hacer,
que tal veneno me das? 1395
Tiempo te queda.

INÉS. Señor,
¿qué importa el hábito pardo
si para siempre le aguardo?

LEONOR. Necia estás.

INÉS. Calla, Leonor.

LEONOR. Por lo menos estas fiestas 1400
has de ver con galas.

INÉS. Mira
que quien por otras suspira
ya no tiene el gusto en éstas.
Galas celestiales son
las que ya mi vida espera. 1405

PEDRO. ¿No basta que yo lo quiera?

INÉS. Obedecerte es razón.

Sale Fabia, *con un rosario y báculo y antojos.*

FABIA. Paz sea en aquesta casa.

PEDRO. Y venga con vos.

FERNANDO.
What nonsense you talk, Rodrigo!

RODRIGO.
It's love that has turned my wits.   *Exeunt.*

[*A room in Don Pedro's house.*]
Enter Don Pedro, Doña Inés, *and* Doña Leonor.

PEDRO.
Don't persist in this foolishness.

INÉS.
You can't shake my purpose.

PEDRO.
Daughter, what are you trying to do, poisoning my life this way? You've got plenty of time.

INÉS.
What difference does it make, sir, if I wear the dark habit now, since I'm expecting soon to put it on for the rest of my life?

LEONOR.
You're silly, Inés.

INÉS.
Be quiet, Leonor.

LEONOR.
At least you will see these festivities dressed in your pretty gowns.

INÉS.
One who sighs for other robes no longer takes pleasure in these. My life now longs for celestial garments.

PEDRO.
Isn't it enough that I want you to wear them?

INÉS.
It's only right, I suppose, to obey you in this.

Enter Fabia, *with rosary, staff, and spectacles.*

FABIA.
Peace be with this house.

PEDRO.
And with you, good mother.

FABIA.   ¿Quién es
    la señora doña Inés,   1410
    que con el Señor se casa?
    ¿Quién es aquella que ya
    tiene su esposo elegida,
    y como a prenda querida
    estos impulsos le da?   1415
PEDRO.   Madre honrada, esta que veis,
    y yo su padre.
FABIA.   ¡Que sea
    muchos años, y ella vea
    el dueño que vos no veis!
    Aunque en el Señor espero   1420
    que os ha de obligar piadoso
    a que acetéis tal esposo,
    que es muy noble caballero.
PEDRO.   Y ¡cómo, madre, si lo es!
FABIA.   Sabiendo que anda a buscar   1425
    quien venga a morigerar
    los verdes años de Inés,
    quien la guíe, quien la muestre
    las sémitas del Señor,
    y al camino del amor   1430
    como a principianta adiestre,
    hice oración en verdad,
    y tal impulso me dio,
    que vengo a ofrecerme yo
    para esta necesidad,   1435
    aunque soy gran pecadora.
PEDRO.   Esta es la mujer, Inés,
    que has menester.
INÉS.   Esta es
    la que he menester agora.
    Madre, abrázame.
FABIA.   Quedito,   1440
    que el silicio me hace mal.
PEDRO.   No he visto humildad igual.
LEONOR. En el rostro trae escrito
    lo que tiene el corazón.

FABIA.

Which one of you is my lady Doña Inés, who is going to marry the Lord? Which one of you has been chosen by Her Husband and inspired, as His dearest love, with these holy impulses?[50]

PEDRO.

Venerable mother, this is the girl, and I'm her father.

FABIA.

May you be so for many years, and may she see the master whom you do not see! Although I trust in the Lord that He will move your pious spirit to accept such a husband, for He is a very noble knight.

PEDRO.

He is indeed, mother, all that you say and more.

FABIA.

Knowing that He seeks someone to restrain Inés's tender youth, someone to guide her, someone to show her the pathways of the Lord and direct her beginner's feet on the road of love, I offered up a prayer from the heart and was filled with such fervor that I've come to offer myself for this purpose, great sinner though I am.

PEDRO.

This is the woman you need, Inés.

INÉS.

She is truly the one I need now. Good mother, embrace me.

FABIA.

Not so tightly, please; my hairshirt pains me.

PEDRO.

I've never seen the like of her humility.

LEONOR.

All that's in her heart is written on her face.

FABIA.	¡Oh, qué gracia! ¡Oh, qué belleza!	1445
	Alcance tu gentileza	
	mi deseo y bendición.	
	¿Tienes oratorio?	
INÉS.	Madre,	
	comienzo a ser buena agora.	
FABIA.	Como yo soy pecadora,	1450
	estoy temiendo a tu padre.	
PEDRO.	No le pienso yo estorbar	
	tan divina vocación.	
FABIA.	¡En vano, infernal dragón,	
	la pensabas devorar!	1455
	No ha de casarse en Medina;	
	monasterio tiene Olmedo;	
	Domine, si tanto puedo,	
	ad iuvandum me festina.	
PEDRO.	Un ángel es la mujer.	1460

Sale Tello, *de gorrón.*

TELLO.	Si con sus hijas está,	
	yo sé que agradecerá	
	que yo me venga a ofrecer.	
	El maestro que buscáis	
	está aquí, señor don Pedro,	1465
	para latín y otras cosas,	
	que dirá después su efeto.	
	Que buscáis un estudiante	
	en la iglesia me dijeron,	
	porque ya desta señora	1470
	se sabe el honesto intento.	
	Aquí he venido a serviros,	
	puesto que soy forastero,	
	si valgo para enseñarla.	
PEDRO.	Ya creo y tengo por cierto,	1475
	viendo que todo se junta,	
	que fue voluntad del cielo.	
	En casa puede quedarse	

1459. ad . . . festina] 1641; a quotation from Psalmus 69:2, but the Vulgate actually reads *ad adjuvandum*.

FABIA.

Oh what charm, what beauty! Blessings on you. May your grace
attain all I desire for you. Do you have an oratory?

INÉS.

Mother, I feel I'm becoming a better person already.

FABIA.

Because I am a miserable sinner, I fear your father's wrath.

PEDRO.

I shall put no obstacles in the way of such a divine calling.

FABIA.

In vain, Satan, oh infernal dragon, did you seek to devour her!
She shall not be married in Medina; there's a convent in
Olmedo. *Domine*, if I can accomplish this, *ad iuvandum me
festina.*[51]

PEDRO.

The woman is an angel.

Enter Tello, *dressed as a poor university student.*[52]

TELLO [*to a servant off*].

If he's with his daughters, I know he'll be pleased that I've come
to offer my services. —My lord Don Pedro, here before you is
the tutor you've been seeking for Latin and sundry other things
that time will reveal. They told me down at the church you
were looking for a student, for people already know about the
chaste intentions of this lady. Although I'm a stranger here in
town, I've come to serve you if I'm worthy to teach her.

PEDRO.

Seeing how everything is falling into place, I'm now convinced
that all this was the will of heaven. The good mother may stay

	la madre, y este mancebo	
	venir a darte lición.	1480
	Concertadlo, mientras vuelvo.	
	¿De dónde es, galán?	
TELLO.	Señor, soy calahorreño.	
PEDRO.	¿Su nombre?	
TELLO.	Martín Peláez.	
PEDRO.	Del Cid debe de ser deudo.	1485
	¿Dónde estudió?	
TELLO.	En La Coruña,	
	y soy por ella maestro.	
PEDRO.	¿Ordenóse?	
TELLO.	Sí, señor,	
	de vísperas.	
PEDRO.	Luego vengo.	
TELLO.	¿Eres Fabia?	
FABIA.	¿No lo ves?	1490
LEONOR.	Y ¿tú Tello?	
INÉS.	¡Amigo Tello!	
LEONOR.	¿Hay mayor bellaquería?	
INÉS.	¿Qué hay de don Alonso?	
TELLO.	¿Puedo	
	fiar de Leonor?	
INÉS.	Bien puedes.	

1482. *¿De dónde es, galán?*] 1641. Two syllables are lacking to complete this line; H changes to *las dos. ¿De dónde es, galán?* J suggests *¿De dónde es, señor galán?*
1489. *vengo*] 1641 does not indicate Pedro's exit here; H does.

in this house, and this young fellow may come here to give you lessons. I'll be back in a moment; in the meantime, arrange matters among you. [*To* Tello.]   Where are you from, young man?

TELLO.

I'm from Calahorra, sir.

PEDRO.

What's your name?

TELLO.

Martín Peláez.[53]

PEDRO.

You must be a relative of the Cid's. Where did you study?

TELLO.

In La Coruña. I have my master's degree from the university there.[54]

PEDRO.

Have you taken holy orders?

TELLO.

Yes, sir. I was ordained to read vespers just a short while ago.[55]

PEDRO.

I'll be back in a minute.

[*Exit* Don Pedro.]

TELLO.

Is that Fabia?

FABIA.

Don't you recognize me?

LEONOR.

And are you Tello?

INÉS.

Oh Tello, my friend!

LEONOR.

Has anybody ever seen such knavery?

INÉS.

What's the news of Don Alonso?

TELLO.

Can I trust Leonor?

INÉS.

Certainly.

LEONOR.   Agraviara Inés mi pecho   1495
          y mi amor, si me tuviera
          su pensamiento encubierto.
TELLO.   Señora, para servirte,
          está don Alonso bueno;
          para las fiestas de mayo,   1500
          tan cerca ya, previniendo
          galas, caballos, jaeces,
          lanza y rejones; que pienso
          que ya le tiemblan los toros.
          Una adarga habemos hecho,   1505
          si se conciertan las cañas,
          como de mi raro ingenio.
          Allá la verás, en fin.
INÉS.   ¿No me ha escrito?
TELLO.   Soy un necio.
          Esta, señora, es la carta.   1510
INÉS.   Bésola de porte y leo.

                    Don Pedro *vuelve.*

PEDRO.   Pues pon el coche, si está
          malo el alazán. ¿Qué es esto?
TELLO.   Tu padre. Haz que lees, y yo
          haré que latín te enseño.   1515
          Dominus.
INÉS.   *Dominus.*
TELLO.   Diga.
INÉS.   ¿Cómo más?
TELLO.   *Dominus meus.*
INÉS.   *Dominus meus.*
TELLO.   Ansí,
          poco a poco irá leyendo.
PEDRO.   ¿Tan presto tomas lición?   1520

LEONOR.

Inés would insult my love for her if she kept her thoughts hidden from me.

TELLO.

Mistress, Don Alonso is well and always at your service. He's getting everything ready—his finery, his horses and their trappings, his pike and lances—for the May festival that's almost upon us. I fancy the bulls are already trembling in anticipation. In case there should be jousting, we've made a buckler with devices and mottoes on it that only my exceptional wit could have conceived.[56] But you'll see it there.

INÉS.

Didn't he write me a letter?

TELLO.

I'm a fool for not remembering it. Here's the letter, mistress.

INÉS.

I kiss it in payment for the postage[57] and shall read it now.

Enter Don Pedro.

PEDRO [*to a servant off*].

Well, get the coach ready if the sorrel is not fit. —What's that you're reading, Inés?

TELLO [*aside to* Doña Inés].

Here's your father. Pretend you're reading and I'll pretend I'm teaching you Latin. —*Dominus*—

INÉS.

Dominus.

TELLO.

Go on and say the rest.

INÉS.

What do you mean, the rest?

TELLO.

Dominus meus.

INÉS.

Dominus meus.

TELLO.

That's the way; little by little you'll learn to read.

PEDRO.

You've started your lessons so soon?

INÉS. Tengo notable deseo.
PEDRO. Basta; que a decir, Inés,
me envía el Ayuntamiento
que salga a las fiestas yo.
INÉS. Muy discretamente han hecho,
pues viene a la fiesta el Rey.
PEDRO. Pues sea, con un concierto;
que has de verlas con Leonor.
INÉS. Madre, dígame si puedo
verlas sin pecar.
FABIA. Pues ¿no?
No escrupulices en eso
como algunos, tan mirlados,
que piensan, de circunspectos,
que en todo ofenden a Dios,
y olvidados de que fueron
hijos de otros, como todos,
cualquiera entretenimiento
que los trabajos olvide
tienen por notable exceso.
Y aunque es justo moderarlos,
doy licencia, por lo menos
para estas fiestas, por ser
iugatoribus paternus.
PEDRO. Pues vamos, que quiero dar
dineros a tu maestro,
y a la madre para un manto.
FABIA. A todos cubra el del cielo.
Y vos, Leonor, ¿no seréis
como vuestra hermana presto?
LEONOR. Sí, madre, porque es muy justo
que tome tan santo ejemplo.

Sale el rey Don Juan, *con acompañamiento, y el* Condestable.

REY. No me traigáis al partir
negocios que despachar.
CONDESTABLE. Contienen sólo firmar;
no has de ocuparte en oír.

1551. *ejemplo*] 1641 omits indication of exit here; H inserts it.

INÉS.

I have a passionate desire to learn.

PEDRO.

Enough of that for now. The Town Council has sent word, Inés, for me to appear at the festival.

INÉS.

They've made a prudent decision, since the King is coming to it.

PEDRO.

Well, so be it; but you must agree to see the festival with Leonor.

INÉS.

Good mother, tell me if I can go without committing a sin.

FABIA.

Why not? Don't be squeamish like some people I know, who are so affected in their devotion and excessively circumspect that they think they are offending God whatever they do; they forget they were born human like everyone else, and they consider any entertainment which distracts them from their work as a great license. Now, even though it's good to moderate one's diversions, I give my permission, at least for these particular festivities, because they're *iugatoribus paternus*.[5 8]

PEDRO.

Well, it's settled then. And I want to give some money to your Latin master and something to the good mother for a mantle.

FABIA.

May the mantle of heaven cover us all. What about you, Leonor, aren't you going to be like your sister soon?

LEONOR.

Oh yes, good mother, for it would be a very wise thing for me to follow so saintly an example.

[*Exeunt.*]

[*The King's residence in Valladolid.*]
Enter King Don Juan, *with his retinue, and the* Lord High Constable.

KING.

Don't bring me business to take care of just when I'm leaving.

CONSTABLE.

You only have to sign these papers; you don't have to listen to their contents.

REY.   Decid con mucha presteza.
CONDESTABLE.   ¿Han de entrar?
REY.   Ahora no.
CONDESTABLE.   Su Santidad concedió
                        lo que pidió Vuestra Alteza
                        por Alcántara, señor.   1560
REY.   Que mudase le pedí
                        el hábito, porque ansí
                        pienso que estará mejor.
CONDESTABLE.   Era aquel traje muy feo.
                        Cruz verde pueden traer.   1565
                        Mucho debo agradecer
                        al Pontífice el deseo
                        que de nuestro aumento muestra,
                        con que irán siempre adelante
                        estas cosas del Infante   1570
                        en cuanto es de parte nuestra.
CONDESTABLE.   Éstas son dos provisiones,
                        y entrambas notables son.
REY.   ¿Qué contienen?
CONDESTABLE.   La razón
                        de diferencia que pones   1575
                        entre los moros y hebreos
                        que en Castilla han de vivir.
REY.   Quiero con esto cumplir,
                        Condestable, los deseos
                        de fray Vicente Ferrer,   1580
                        que lo ha deseado tanto.
CONDESTABLE.   Es un hombre docto y santo.
REY.   Resolví con él ayer
                        que en cualquiera reino mío
                        donde mezclados están,   1585
                        a manera de gabán
                        traiga un tabardo el judío
                        con una señal en él,
                        y un verde capuz el moro.

KING.

Well, say what you must quickly.

CONSTABLE.

Should the messengers come in?[59]

KING.

Not right now.

CONSTABLE.

His Holiness has granted Your Highness's petition with respect to the Order of Alcántara,[60] my lord.

KING.

I asked him to change their habit because it will be much finer as I've requested it.[61]

CONSTABLE.

The old habit was very ugly.

KING.

Now they can wear a green cross on their habit. I owe much gratitude to the Pope for the good will he has demonstrated toward the increase of our estates. The Infante's affairs will always prosper, inasmuch as the Pope is on our side.[62]

CONSTABLE.

Here are two royal orders, both of them notable.

KING.

What do they say?

CONSTABLE.

The first details the different modes of dress you have imposed on the Moors and Jews who live in Castile.

KING.

This is designed, Constable, to carry out the wishes of Friar Vicente Ferrer, who has desired such an arrangement so intensely.

CONSTABLE.

He is a learned and holy man.

KING.

I resolved with him yesterday that in any province of mine where the three religions are intermingled, the Jew's cloak must be a tabard with a special device on it, and the Moor must wear a green cowl. Let Christians maintain the proper decorum and

	Tenga el cristiano el decoro	1590
	que es justo: apártese dél;	
	que con esto tendrán miedo	
	los que su nobleza infaman.	
CONDESTABLE.	A don Alonso, que llaman	
	el caballero de Olmedo,	1595
	hace Vuestra Alteza aquí	
	merced de un hábito.	
REY.	Es hombre	
	de notable fama y nombre.	
	En esta villa le vi	
	cuando se casó mi hermana.	1600
CONDESTABLE.	Pues pienso que determina,	
	por servirte, ir a Medina	
	a las fiestas de mañana.	
REY.	Decidle que fama emprenda	
	en el arte militar,	1605
	porque yo le pienso honrar	
	con la primera encomienda. *Vanse.*	

Sale Don Alonso.

ALONSO.	¡Ay, riguroso estado,	
	ausencia mi enemiga,	
	que dividiendo el alma,	1610
	puedes dejar la vida!	
	¡Cuán bien por tus efetos	
	te llaman muerte viva,	
	pues das vida al deseo	
	y matas a la vista!	1615
	¡Oh, cuán piadosa fueras,	
	si al partir de Medina	
	la vida me quitaras	
	como el alma me quitas!	
	En ti, Medina, vive	1620
	aquella Inés divina,	
	que es honra de la corte	
	y gloria de la villa.	
	Sus alabanzas cantan	
	las aguas fugitivas,	1625

stay away from them; this new provision will instill fear in those who mingle too freely and thus discredit their noble Christian blood.[63]

CONSTABLE.

In the second writ Your Highness grants a habit[64] to Don Alonso, whom they call the "Knight of Olmedo."

KING.

He is a man of excellent reputation and high renown. I saw him here in this city at my sister's wedding.[65]

CONSTABLE.

Well, I think he has determined to serve you by appearing in the festival at Medina tomorrow.

KING.

Tell him to seek ever more fame in the military arts, for I plan to honor him with the first fief belonging to his order which becomes available.   *Exeunt.*

[*A room in Don Alonso's house in Olmedo.*]
Enter Don Alonso.

ALONSO.

Oh harsh condition, this cruel absence which severs my soul in two yet leaves me still with life! How right they are who, seeing your effects, call you a living death, for you give life to desire while killing sight. Oh how compassionate you would have been if, when I left Medina, you had taken away my life as you took away my soul! In you, Medina, lives the divine Inés, honor of the court and glory of the town. The flowing waters sing her praise, as do the birds that hear her and the

las aves que la escuchan,
las flores que la imitan.
Es tan bella que tiene
envidia de sí misma,
pudiendo estar segura   1630
que el mismo sol la envidia;
pues no la ve más bella,
por su dorada cinta,
ni cuando viene a España,
ni cuando va a las Indias.   1635
Yo merecí quererla.
¡Dichosa mi osadía,
que es merecer sus penas
calificar mis dichas!
Cuando pudiera verla,   1640
adorarla y servirla,
la fuerza del secreto
de tanto bien me priva.
Cuando mi amor no fuera
de fe tan pura y limpia,   1645
las perlas de sus ojos
mi muerte solicitan.
Llorando por mi ausencia
Inés quedó aquel día,
que sus lágrimas fueron   1650
de sus palabras firma.
Bien sabe aquella noche
que pudiera ser mía.
Cobarde amor, ¿qué aguardas,
cuando respetos miras?   1655
¡Ay, Dios, qué gran desdicha,
partir el alma y dividir la vida!

                   Sale Tello.

TELLO.   ¿Merezco ser bien llegado?
ALONSO.   No sé si diga que sí,
que me has tenido sin mí   1660
con lo mucho que has tardado.
TELLO.   Si por tu remedio ha sido,
¿en qué me puedes culpar?

flowers that imitate her. She is so lovely that she envies her own self, even though she might be sure that the very sun does envy her; for he sees no one more lovely in all the golden ribbon of his course, neither when he comes to Spain nor when he goes to the Indies.[66] And I had the tremendous fortune to love her! How happy was my daring, for to describe my joy then is to justify my pain now. When I might have seen her, adored her, served her, the need for secrecy deprives me of such happiness. If my love were not so pure and chaste in its faith, the pearls which fell from her eyes would demand my death. Inés wept that day because I was leaving; her tears confirmed her words. That night could testify that she might have been mine. Oh cowardly love, what are you waiting for when you hold back out of respect for honor? Oh God, how great a misfortune: my soul separated, my life divided![67]

Enter Tello.

TELLO.
Do I deserve a welcome?

ALONSO.
I don't know whether you do or not. You've been so slow I've nearly gone out of my mind.

TELLO.
It was all for your good, so how can you blame me?

ALONSO.   ¿Quién me puede remediar,
             si no es a quien yo le pido?   1665
             ¿No me escribe Inés?
TELLO.   Aquí
             te traigo cartas de Inés.
ALONSO.   Pues hablarásme después
             en lo que has hecho por mí.
             Lea. «Señor mío, después que os partis-
             tes no he vivido; que sois tan cruel, que
             aun no me dejáis vida cuando os vais.»
TELLO.   ¿No lees más?
ALONSO.   No.
TELLO.   ¿Por qué?   1670
ALONSO.   Porque manjar tan süave
             de una vez no se me acabe.
             Hablemos de Inés.
TELLO.   Llegué
             con media sotana y guantes,
             que parecía de aquellos   1675
             que hacen en solos los cuellos
             ostentación de estudiantes.
             Encajé salutación,
             verbosa filatería,
             dando a la bachillería   1680
             dos piensos de discreción;
             y volviendo el rostro, vi
             a Fabia.
ALONSO.   Espera, que leo
             otro poco; que el deseo
             me tiene fuera de mí.   1685
             Lea. «Todo lo que dejastes ordenado se
             hizo; sólo no se hizo que viviese yo sin
             vos, porque no lo dejasteis ordenado.»
TELLO.   ¿Es aquí contemplación?
ALONSO.   Dime cómo hizo Fabia
             lo que dice Inés.

ALONSO.

Who can help me unless it be she whose aid I beg? Hasn't Inés written me?

TELLO.

Here are the letters from Inés.

ALONSO.

Later you can tell me what you've done for me. (*Reads.*) "My Lord, since you went away, I have not lived, for you are so cruel that you do not even leave me my life when you depart."

TELLO.

Aren't you going to read any more?

ALONSO.

No.

TELLO.

Why not?

ALONSO.

I don't want so delicate a dish to be finished in one bite. Let's talk about Inés instead.

TELLO.

I appeared with a short cassock and gloves, looking like one of those fellows who put on a show of being students by the miserable collars they wear.[68] I offered the most flowery of salutations, mixing two measures of wit with pedantic prattle; then I turned my head and saw Fabia—

ALONSO.

Wait and let me read a little more, for desire is driving me mad. (*Reads.*) "All you ordered has been done; it has only not been arranged that I should live without you, because that you did not order."

TELLO.

Is this what they call mystic ecstasy?

ALONSO.

Tell me how Fabia did all the things Inés says.

TELLO.　　　　　　　　　　Tan sabia
　　　　y con tanta discreción,
　　　　　　melindre y hipocresía,　　　　　　　　　1690
　　　　que me dieron que temer
　　　　algunos que suelo ver
　　　　cabizbajos todo el día.
　　　　　　De hoy más quedaré advertido
　　　　de lo que se ha de creer　　　　　　　　　　　1695
　　　　de una hipócrita mujer
　　　　y un ermitaño fingido.
　　　　　　Pues si me vieras a mí
　　　　con el semblante mirlado,
　　　　dijeras que era traslado　　　　　　　　　　　1700
　　　　de un reverendo alfaquí.
　　　　　　Creyóme el viejo, aunque en él
　　　　se ve de un Catón retrato.

ALONSO.　Espera, que ha mucho rato
　　　　que no he mirado el papel.　　　　　　　　　1705

　　　Lea. «Daos prisa a venir, para que sepáis
　　　cómo quedo cuando os partís y cómo es-
　　　toy cuando volvéis.»

TELLO.　　　　¿Hay otra estación aquí?

ALONSO.　En fin, tú hallaste lugar
　　　　para entrar y para hablar.

TELLO.　Estudiaba Inés en ti;
　　　　　　que eras el latín, señor,　　　　　　　　1710
　　　　y la lición que aprendía.

ALONSO.　Leonor ¿qué hacía?

TELLO.　　　　　　　　　　　Tenía
　　　　envidia de tanto amor,
　　　　　　porque se daba a entender
　　　　que de ser amado eres　　　　　　　　　　　1715
　　　　digno: que muchas mujeres
　　　　quieren porque ven querer;
　　　　　　que en siendo un hombre querido
　　　　de alguna con grande afeto,

1719. *afeto*] H; 1641 spells *afecto*, but the pronunciation was as indicated by H in order to rhyme with *secreto*.

TELLO.

She did it all so wisely and with such discretion, such prudery, such hypocrisy that I began to be afraid of certain people I see going around with their heads meekly bowed every day. From now on I'll be on my guard about how much credit should be given to a hypocritical woman and a feigned hermit. For if you had seen me with my solemn countenance, you would have said I was the very image of a reverend Moslem sage. The old man believed me, even though he's the perfect picture of a stern Cato.

ALONSO.

Wait; it's been a long time since I've looked at the paper. (*Reads.*) "Make haste to come, so that you may know how I'm left when you depart and how I am when you return."

TELLO.

Shall we pray again here?

ALONSO.

In short, you found a way to get in and to speak to her.

TELLO.

Inés's whole study is you; you were the Latin, master, and you the lesson that she was learning.

ALONSO.

What was Leonor doing?

TELLO.

She was envious of so much love, because it was clear to her that you are worthy of being loved, for many women fall in love because they see others are in love. And when a man is worshipped by some woman, they think there's some secret

	piensan que hay algún secreto	1720
	en aquel hombre escondido;	
	y engáñanse, porque son	
	correspondencias de estrellas.	
ALONSO.	Perdonadme, manos bellas,	
	que leo el postrer renglón.	1725

ALONSO.   Perdonadme, manos bellas,
que leo el postrer renglón.   1725
Lea. «Dicen que viene el Rey a Medina,
y dicen verdad, pues habéis de venir vos,
que sois rey mío.»
Acabóseme el papel.
TELLO.   Todo en el mundo se acaba.
ALONSO.   Poco dura el bien.
TELLO.   En fin,
le has leído por jornadas.
ALONSO.   Espera, que aquí a la margen   1730
vienen dos o tres palabras.
Lea. «Poneos esa banda al cuello.
¡Ay, si yo fuera la banda!»
TELLO.   ¡Bien dicho, por Dios, y entrar
con doña Inés en la plaza!   1735
ALONSO.   ¿Dónde está la banda, Tello?
TELLO.   A mí no me han dado nada.
ALONSO.   ¿Cómo no?
TELLO.   Pues ¿qué me has dado?
ALONSO.   Ya te entiendo: luego saca
a tu elección un vestido.   1740
TELLO.   Ésta es la banda.
ALONSO.   Estremada.
TELLO.   Tales manos la bordaron.
ALONSO.   Demos orden que me parta.
Pero ¡ay, Tello!

charm hidden in the man; but they are deceived, because their stars have brought them together.[69]

ALONSO.

Oh lovely hands, pardon me while I read the last lines you've written. (*Reads.*) "They say the King is coming to Medina, and they speak the truth, for you will come, and you are my king." The note is ended.

TELLO.

Everything in the world ends.

ALONSO.

Good things last so short a time.

TELLO.

And so you've read the letter in four acts.

ALONSO.

Wait a moment. There're two or three words written in the margin. (*Reads.*) "Put this sash around your neck. Oh would that I were the sash!"

TELLO.

What a fine idea, by heaven. Then you could ride into the plaza with Inés wrapped around your neck!

ALONSO.

Where's the sash, Tello?

TELLO.

Nobody's given me anything.

ALONSO.

How is that?

TELLO.

Well, what have you given me, master?

ALONSO.

I get the idea; you can choose any suit you like from my wardrobe right now.

TELLO.

Here's the sash.

ALONSO.

It is superb.

TELLO.

Just like the hands that embroidered it.

ALONSO.

Let's give the order for my departure. But alas, Tello!

TELLO.   ¿Qué tenemos?
ALONSO.   De decirte me olvidaba   1745
unos sueños que he tenido.
TELLO.   ¿Agora en sueños reparas?
ALONSO.   No los creo, claro está;
pero dan pena.
TELLO.   Eso basta.
ALONSO.   No falta quien llama a algunos   1750
revelaciones del alma.
TELLO.   ¿Qué te puede suceder
en una cosa tan llana
como quererte casar?
ALONSO.   Hoy, Tello, al salir el alba,   1755
con la inquietud de la noche,
me levanté de la cama,
abrí la ventana aprisa,
y mirando flores y aguas
que adornan nuestro jardín,   1760
sobre una verde retama
veo ponerse un jilguero,
cuyas esmaltadas alas
con lo amarillo añadían
flores a las verdes ramas.   1765
Y estando al aire trinando
de la pequeña garganta
con naturales pasajes
las quejas enamoradas,
sale un azor de un almendro,   1770
adonde escondido estaba,
y como eran en los dos
tan desiguales las armas,
tiñó de sangre las flores,
plumas al aire derrama.   1775
Al triste chillido, Tello,
débiles ecos del aura
respondieron, y, no lejos,
lamentando su desgracia,
su esposa, que en un jazmín   1780
la tragedia viendo estaba.

TELLO.

What's wrong?

ALONSO.

I forgot to tell you some strange dreams[70] I've had.

TELLO.

Don't tell me you're paying attention to dreams now.

ALONSO.

I don't believe in them, of course, but they cause me pain.

TELLO.

Well, that's enough.

ALONSO.

There are those who call some of them revelations of the soul.

TELLO.

What can possibly happen to you in such a simple matter as wanting to get married?

ALONSO.

This morning, Tello, when dawn came after a restless night, I got up from my bed and opened the window quickly. As I looked at the flowers and fountains that adorn our garden, I saw a goldfinch light on a bush of green broom, its bright wings lending yellow flowers to the green branches. And while its small throat trilled forth its amorous complaints with untaught art, a goshawk flew out of an almond tree where it was hiding. Since their arms were so unequal, the goldfinch stained the flowers with its blood and scattered feathers on the air. Faint echoes from the passing breeze answered its mournful cries, and not far away, perched on a jasmine from which she viewed the tragedy, his mate lamented the finch's unhappy fate. And I,

Yo, midiendo con los sueños
estos avisos del alma,
apenas puedo alentarme;
que con saber que son falsas   1785
todas estas cosas, tengo
tan perdida la esperanza,
que no me aliento a vivir.

TELLO.   Mal a doña Inés le pagas
aquella heroica firmeza   1790
con que atrevida contrasta
los golpes de la fortuna.
Ven a Medina, y no hagas
caso de sueños ni agüeros,
cosas a la fe contrarias.   1795
Lleva el ánimo que sueles,
caballos, lanzas y galas,
mata de envidia los hombres,
mata de amores las damas.
Doña Inés ha de ser tuya   1800
a pesar de cuantos tratan
dividiros a los dos.

ALONSO.   Bien dices, Inés me aguarda:
vamos a Medina alegres.
Las penas anticipadas   1805
dicen que matan dos veces,
y a mí sola Inés me mata,
no como pena, que es gloria.

TELLO.   Tú me verás en la plaza
hincar de rodillas toros   1810
delante de sus ventanas.

Fin del segundo acto del *Caballero de Olmedo*.

comparing my dreams with the warnings of my own soul, can scarcely feel encouraged; for even though I know all these things are false, hope has so abandoned me that I have no heart to live.

TELLO.

You ill repay Doña Inés for the heroic steadfastness with which she boldly meets the blows of fortune. Go to Medina, and pay no attention to dreams and omens; belief in them is contrary to our faith. Arm yourself with your accustomed courage; take your horses, lances, finest clothes; slay men with envy of you and ladies for love of you. Doña Inés will be yours despite all those who seek to separate you.

ALONSO.

You are right. Inés is waiting for me. Let's go to Medina merrily. The pains we anticipate kill us twice, they say; and Inés alone can slay me, and not from pain, for she is glory.

TELLO.

In the plaza you'll see me force bulls to kneel down before her windows.[71]

End of the second act of *The Knight of Olmedo*.

ACTO TERCERO

Suenen atabales y entren con lacayos y rejones
Don Rodrigo y Don Fernando.

RODRIGO.   Poca dicha.
FERNANDO.   Malas suertes.
RODRIGO.   ¡Qué pesar!
FERNANDO.   ¿Qué se ha de hacer?
RODRIGO.   Brazo, ya no puede ser
                 que en servir a Inés aciertes.   1815
FERNANDO.   Corrido estoy.
RODRIGO.   Yo, turbado.
FERNANDO.   Volvamos a porfiar.
RODRIGO.   Es imposible acertar
                 un hombre tan desdichado.
                 Para el de Olmedo, en efeto,   1820
                 guardó suertes la fortuna.
FERNANDO.   No ha errado el hombre ninguna.
RODRIGO.   ¡Que la ha de errar os prometo!
FERNANDO.   Un hombre favorecido,
                 Rodrigo, todo lo acierta.   1825
RODRIGO.   Abrióle el amor la puerta,
                 y a mí, Fernando, el olvido.
                 Fuera desto, un forastero
                 luego se lleva los ojos.

ACT III

[*Outside the plaza of Medina.*]
Drums sound, and Don Rodrigo *and* Don Fernando *enter with
their* lackeys *and lances.*

RODRIGO.
I've had poor luck.

FERNANDO.
Bad thrusts.[72]

RODRIGO.
What unhappiness!

FERNANDO.
But what's to be done about it?

RODRIGO.
It's no longer possible for my arm to do anything right in Inés's
service!

FERNANDO.
I'm ashamed.

RODRIGO.
And I'm dismayed.

FERNANDO.
Let's go back and try again.

RODRIGO.
It's impossible for so unlucky a man to be successful. In truth,
fortune has kept all the good thrusts for that fellow from
Olmedo.

FERNANDO.
The man hasn't missed a single one.

RODRIGO.
But he will yet, I promise you!

FERNANDO.
The man who is favored in love is successful at everything,
Rodrigo.

RODRIGO.
Love showed him the way, Fernando, and disdain is my only
guide. Besides that, a stranger attracts attention immediately.

FERNANDO.   Vos tenéis justos enojos.   1830
            Él es galán caballero,
            mas no para escurecer
            los hombres que hay en Medina.
RODRIGO.   La patria me desatina;
            mucho parece mujer   1835
            en que lo propio desprecia
            y de lo ajeno se agrada.
FERNANDO.   De siempre ingrata culpada
            son ejemplos Roma y Grecia.

                Dentro, ruido de pretales y voces.

[HOMBRE] 1.º   ¡Brava suerte!
[HOMBRE] 2.º   ¡Con qué gala   1840
            quebró el rejón!
FERNANDO.   ¿Qué aguardamos?
            Tomemos caballos.
RODRIGO.   Vamos.
[HOMBRE] 1.º ¡Nadie en el mundo le iguala!
FERNANDO.   ¿Oyes esa voz?
RODRIGO.   No puedo
            sufrirlo.
FERNANDO.   Aún no lo encareces.   1845
[HOMBRE] 2.º ¡Vitor setecientas veces
            el caballero de Olmedo!
RODRIGO.   ¿Qué suerte quieres que aguarde,
            Fernando, con estas voces?
FERNANDO.   Es vulgo, ¿no le conoces?   1850
[HOMBRE] 1.º ¡Dios te guarde, Dios te guarde!

1838. *De siempre ingrata*] 1641; *De ser de ingrata* H.

FERNANDO.

You have every right to be angry. He is a gallant gentleman but not so excellent as to blot out all the men in Medina.

RODRIGO.

That my own town should act this way infuriates me. It's very like a fickle woman, scorning whatever belongs to it and showing enthusiasm for what is alien.

FERNANDO.

It's always been that way. Rome and Greece are classical examples of ingratitude.

Offstage the noise of the snapping of horses' leather breastplates and shouting voices.

FIRST MAN [*off*].

A fine thrust!

SECOND MAN [*off*].

How elegantly he broke the lance![73]

FERNANDO.

What are we waiting for? Let's get our horses.

RODRIGO.

Let's go.

FIRST MAN [*off*].

He has no equal in the whole world!

FERNANDO.

Did you hear that?

RODRIGO.

I can't bear it.

FERNANDO.

You're not exaggerating the situation.

SECOND MAN [*off*].

Seven hundred *bravos* for the knight from Olmedo!

RODRIGO.

What kind of luck in the fight can I expect, Fernando, with that crowd?

FERNANDO.

They're ignorant peasants. Don't you know that?

FIRST MAN [*off*].

God keep you! God keep you!

RODRIGO.	¿Qué más dijeran al Rey?
	Mas bien hacen: digan, rueguen
	que hasta el fin sus dichas lleguen.
FERNANDO.	Fue siempre bárbara ley 1855
	seguir aplauso vulgar
	las novedades.
RODRIGO.	Él viene
	a mudar caballo.
FERNANDO.	Hoy tiene
	la fortuna en su lugar.

Salen Tello, *con rejón y librea, y* Don Alonso.

TELLO.	¡Valientes suertes, por Dios! 1860
ALONSO.	Dame, Tello, el alazán.
TELLO.	Todos el lauro nos dan.
ALONSO.	¿A los dos, Tello?
TELLO.	A los dos;
	que tú a caballo, y yo a pie,
	nos habemos igualado. 1865
ALONSO.	¡Qué bravo, Tello, has andado!
TELLO.	Seis toros desjarreté,
	como si sus piernas fueran
	rábanos de mi lugar.
FERNANDO.	Volvamos, Rodrigo, a entrar, 1870
	que por dicha nos esperan,
	aunque os parece que no.
RODRIGO.	A vos, don Fernando, sí;
	a mí no, si no es que a mí
	me esperan para que yo 1875
	haga suertes que me afrenten,
	o que algún toro me mate,
	o me arrastre o me maltrate
	donde con risa lo cuenten.

Vanse los dos.

TELLO.	Aquéllos te están mirando. 1880

RODRIGO.

What more could they say to the King? But they do well: let them talk, let them pray that his good fortune continue to the end.

FERNANDO.

It's always been the monstrous rule that the applause of the mob should be given to anything new.

RODRIGO.

He's coming out to change horses.

FERNANDO.

Today he has fortune on his side.

Enter Tello, *with lance and livery, and* Don Alonso.

TELLO.

Wonderful thrusts, as God is my witness!

ALONSO.

Give me the sorrel, Tello.

TELLO.

Everybody says we should get the prize.

ALONSO.

Both of us, Tello?

TELLO.

Both of us. We've fought equally well, you on horseback and me on foot.

ALONSO.

How bold you've been, Tello!

TELLO.

I killed six bulls by cutting their legs off as if I were snipping radishes in my village.

FERNANDO.

Let's go back in, Rodrigo; maybe they're waiting for us, even though you may not think so.

RODRIGO.

They're waiting for you, Fernando, but not for me, unless they're waiting for me to make thrusts that dishonor me, or for some bull to kill me, or drag me, or gore me in some shameful place so they can laugh about it.

Exeunt [Don Rodrigo *and* Don Fernando].

TELLO.

Those two were staring at you.

ALONSO.   Ya los he visto envidiosos
de mis dichas, y aun celosos
de mirarme a Inés mirando.
TELLO.   ¡Bravos favores te ha hecho
con la risa! Que la risa   1885
es lengua muda que avisa
de lo que pasa en el pecho.
No pasabas vez ninguna
que arrojar no se quería
del balcón.
ALONSO.   ¡Ay, Inés mía!   1890
¡Si quisiese la fortuna
que a mis padres les llevase
tal prenda de sucesión!
TELLO.   Sí haras, como la ocasión
deste don Rodrigo pase;   1895
porque satisfecho estoy
de que Inés por ti se abrasa.
ALONSO.   Fabia se ha quedado en casa;
mientras una vuelta doy
a la plaza, ve corriendo   1900
y di que esté prevenida
Inés, porque en mi partida
la pueda hablar, advirtiendo
que si esta noche no fuese
a Olmedo, me han de contar   1905
mis padres por muerto; y dar
ocasión, si no los viese,
a esta pena, no es razón.
Tengan buen sueño, que es justo.
TELLO.   Bien dices; duerman con gusto,   1910
pues es forzosa ocasión
de temer y de esperar.
ALONSO.   Yo entro.   *Vase* Don Alonso.

1908. *no es razón*] 1641; *y no es razón* H.
1913. *entro*] H; 1641 puts Don Alonso's exit after *esperar* in vs. 1912.

ALONSO.

I've already noticed that they were envious of my good luck and even jealous to see me looking at Inés.

TELLO.   `

She's bestowed fine favors on you with her laughter and smiles, for smiles are a wordless tongue which signals what is happening in the heart. You didn't pass by a single time when she didn't seem to want to throw herself down from the balcony.

ALONSO.

Oh my Inés! If it should only be fortune's will that I might take to my parents so fine a pledge that their succession was assured!

TELLO.

And so you will as soon as Don Rodrigo's day is over, because I'm sure Inés is burning with love for you.

ALONSO.

Fabia stayed at home today; while I ride round the plaza, run and tell her that Inés should be ready so I can speak to her before I leave. Let her know that if I don't return to Olmedo tonight, my parents will think I'm dead, and it wouldn't be right for me to give them cause for such sorrow by failing to see them. They should rest comfortably, that's only fair.

TELLO.

You're right. Let them sleep well. Your failure to return home on this occasion would surely make them anxious and fearful.

ALONSO.

I'm going in again.   *Exit* Don Alonso.

TELLO. ¡Guárdete el cielo!
Pues puedo hablar sin recelo,
a Fabia quiero llegar.   1915
Traigo cierto pensamiento
para coger la cadena
a esta vieja, aunque con pena
de su astuto entendimiento.
No supo Circe, Medea,   1920
ni Hécate, lo que ella sabe;
tendrá en el alma una llave
que de treinta vueltas sea.
Mas no hay maestra mejor
que decirle que la quiero,   1925
que es el remedio primero
para una mujer mayor;
que con dos razones tiernas
de amores y voluntad,
presumen de mocedad   1930
y piensan que son eternas.
Acabóse. Llego, llamo.
Fabia... Pero soy un necio;
que sabrá que el oro precio
y que los años desamo,   1935
porque se lo ha de decir
el de las patas de gallo.

Sale Fabia.

FABIA. ¡Jesús, Tello! ¿Aquí te hallo?
¡Qué buen modo de servir
a don Alonso! ¿Qué es esto?   1940
¿Qué ha sucedido?
TELLO.   No alteres
lo venerable, pues eres
causa de venir tan presto;
que por verte anticipé
de don Alonso un recado.   1945

1931. *eternas*] 1641; H indicates an exit for Tello here, making a new scene begin at *Acabóse*. Either solution is possible; choice between them would depend on how stage was set.

TELLO.

May heaven protect you! —Now that I'm alone, I can talk without fear. I'd like to see Fabia too. I've got an idea about getting the chain away from the old woman, though I'm afraid of her sharp wits. Circe, Medea, and Hecate didn't know as much as she does. It must take a key with thirty wards on it to unlock the secrets of her soul. But there's no better master key than telling her I love her, which is the best medicine to use on old women. Two tender phrases about love and desire, and they boast they're spring chickens and think they're immortal.

[*Exit* Tello.] [74]

[*Exterior view of Don Pedro's house.*]
[*Enter* Tello.]

TELLO.

Well, here I am. I'll go to the door. I knock. Fabia— But I'm a fool; she's going to know that it's the gold I prize and her years that I despise, because the rooster-footed devil is bound to tell her all about it.

Enter Fabia [*from Don Pedro's house*].

FABIA.

For heaven's sake, Tello! What a place to find you! This is no way to serve Don Alonso! What's this all about? What's happened?

TELLO.

Don't get your venerable dander up, because you're my reason for coming so soon; just to see you I came ahead of time with a message from Don Alonso.

FABIA.	¿Cómo ha andado?
TELLO.	Bien ha andado,
	porque yo le acompañé.
FABIA.	¡Estremado fanfarrón!
TELLO.	Pregúntalo al Rey, verás
	cuál de los dos hizo más; 1950
	que se echaba del balcón
	cada vez que yo pasaba.
FABIA.	¡Bravo favor!
TELLO.	Más quisiera
	los tuyos.
FABIA.	¡Oh, quién te viera!
TELLO.	Esa hermosura bastaba 1955
	para que yo fuera Orlando.
	¿Toros de Medina a mí?
	¡Vive el cielo!, que les di
	reveses, desjarretando,
	de tal aire, de tal casta, 1960
	en medio del regocijo,
	que hubo toro que me dijo:
	«Basta, señor Tello, basta.»
	«No basta», le dije yo,
	y eché de un tajo volado 1965
	una pierna en un tejado.
FABIA.	Y ¿cuántas tejas quebró?
TELLO.	Eso al dueño, que no a mí.
	Dile, Fabia, a tu señora
	que ese mozo que la adora 1970
	vendrá a despedirse aquí;
	que es fuerza volverse a casa,
	porque no piensen que es muerto
	sus padres. Esto te advierto.
	Y porque la fiesta pasa 1975
	sin mí, y el Rey me ha de echar
	menos, que en efeto soy
	su toricida, me voy
	a dar materia al lugar
	de vítores y de aplauso, 1980
	si me das algún favor.
FABIA.	¿Yo favor?

FABIA.

How did things go with him at the fiesta?

TELLO.

He got along fine because I was with him.

FABIA.

You consummate braggart!

TELLO.

Just ask the King himself and you'll see which of us two did the most; he nearly threw himself down from the balcony every time I passed by.

FABIA.

My, what a rare mark of favor he showed you!

TELLO.

I'd much prefer your favors.

FABIA.

How I wish I had seen you!

TELLO.

Your beauty served to turn me into a veritable Roland. What did Medina's bulls matter to me? By heaven, as I chopped off their legs, I gave them backhand thrusts with the sword so debonairly, so elegantly, in the midst of all the jubilation, that one bull said to me, "That's enough, master Tello, that's enough." "It's not enough," I replied, and with one swift cut I sent one of his legs flying up onto a roof.

FABIA.

And how many tiles did it break?

TELLO.

That's the owner's problem, not mine. Fabia, tell your mistress that that young man who adores her will come here to say goodbye to her. He has to return home so his parents won't think he is dead. And because the festival is going on without me and the King's going to miss me, for in truth I'm his bull-slayer, I'm going to return to provide the town with a reason for *bravos* and applause—that is, if you'll only give me a favor.

FABIA.

You want me to give you a favor?

TELLO.	Paga mi amor.
FABIA.	¿Que yo tus hazañas causo?
	Basta, que no lo sabía.
	¿Qué te agrada más?
TELLO.	Tus ojos.
FABIA.	Pues daréte sus antojos.
TELLO.	Por caballo, Fabia mía,
	quedo confirmado ya.
FABIA.	Propio favor de lacayo.
TELLO.	Más castaño soy que bayo.
FABIA.	Mira cómo andas allá,
	que esto de *ne nos inducas*
	suelen causar los refrescos;
	no te quite los greguescos
	algún mozo de San Lucas;
	que será notable risa,
	Tello, que, donde lo vea
	todo el mundo, un toro sea
	sumiller de tu camisa.
TELLO.	Lo atacado y el cuidado
	volverán por mi decoro.
FABIA.	Para un desgarro de un toro,
	¿Qué importa estar atacado?
TELLO.	Que no tengo a toros miedo.
FABIA.	Los de Medina hacen riza,
	porque tienen ojeriza
	con los lacayos de Olmedo.
TELLO.	Como ésos ha derribado,
	Fabia, este brazo español.

1985

1990

1995

2000

2005

1992. ne nos inducas] H; *no nos inducas* 1641.

TELLO.

Reward my love.

FABIA.

So I'm the inspiration of all your daring feats? Wonders never cease! I certainly didn't know it. What do you like most about me?

TELLO.

Your eyes.

FABIA.

Well then, I'll give you my eyeglasses.

TELLO.

Oh my Fabia, with those blinders on, I'll certainly look like the stallion I am.

FABIA.

Well, blinders are a fitting token of love for a lackey like you who takes care of horses.

TELLO.

I warn you I'm more of a fiery chestnut than a gentle bay.

FABIA.

Take care back there in the bullring; trying one's luck once too often is what leads people to pray "lead us not into temptation." Don't let one of those bulls[75] rip your trousers off. It would be a big joke, Tello, if right there in public a bull should become your royal valet and undress you.

TELLO.

I've got buttons to hold my trousers up, and they and my own caution will guard my decency.

FABIA.

When a bull rips your pants, what does it help to have them buttoned on?

TELLO.

I tell you I'm not afraid of bulls.

FABIA.

The bulls of Medina will tear you up. They have a grudge against lackeys from Olmedo.

TELLO.

This Spanish arm has chopped down lots of ill-tempered beasts like that, Fabia.

FABIA.   ¡Más que te ha de dar el sol   2010
               adonde nunca te ha dado!

Ruido de plaza y grita, y digan dentro:

[HOMBRE] 1.º   Cayó don Rodrigo.
ALONSO.   ¡Afuera!
[HOMBRE] 2.º   ¡Qué gallardo, qué animoso
               don Alonso le socorre!
[HOMBRE] 1.º   Ya se apea don Alonso.   2015
[HOMBRE] 2.º   ¡Qué valientes cuchilladas!
[HOMBRE] 1.º   ¡Hizo pedazos el toro!

Salgan los dos, y Don Alonso *teniéndole.*

ALONSO.   Aquí tengo yo caballo;
          que los nuestros van furiosos
          discurriendo por la plaza.   2020
          Ánimo.
RODRIGO.   Con vos le cobro.
          La caída ha sido grande.
ALONSO.   Pues no será bien que al coso
          volváis; aquí habrá criados
          que os sirvan, porque yo torno   2025
          a la plaza. Perdonadme,
          porque cobrar es forzoso
          el caballo que dejé.

Vase, y sale Don Fernando.

FERNANDO.   ¿Qué es esto? ¡Rodrigo, y solo!
            ¿Cómo estáis?
RODRIGO.   Mala caída,   2030
            mal suceso, malo todo;
            pero más deber la vida
            a quien me tiene celoso
            y a quien la muerte deseo.

2010. ¡*Más* ... *dado*!] 1641. So punctuated, *más que* means "although"; R
punctuates *Mas ¿qué, te ha de dar el sol / adonde nunca te ha dado?* The line then
means, "But what an idea! Is the sun going to shine then on those parts of you it's never
seen before?" H adds here the indication that Fabia and Tello leave the stage.

2019. *nuestros*] 1641; *vuestros* (yours) R.

FABIA.

Even so, the sun is bound to shine on your private parts where it has never shone before!

[*Exeunt.*]

[*Outside the plaza of Medina.*]
Noise and shouting from the plaza; voices are heard from offstage.

FIRST MAN [*off*].

Don Rodrigo has fallen!

ALONSO [*off*].

Let's get him out!

SECOND MAN [*off*].

How gallantly and bravely Don Alonso goes to his aid!

FIRST MAN [*off*].

Don Alonso is getting off his horse now.

SECOND MAN [*off*].

What marvellous sword thrusts!

FIRST MAN [*off*].

He's made mincemeat of the bull!

Enter Don Alonso, *supporting* Don Rodrigo.

ALONSO.

I've got another horse out here. Ours are running wildly around the plaza. Take heart.

RODRIGO.

Your help has given me strength again. That was a serious fall.

ALONSO.

It's not a good idea for you to return to the ring; there must be servants around here who can aid you, because I'm going to return to the plaza. Pardon me, but I must recover the horse I left there.

He goes out, and Don Fernando *enters.*

FERNANDO.

What's this? Rodrigo, you're here alone! How are you?

RODRIGO.

A bad fall, a bad turn of events, everything is bad! But the worst of all is to owe my life to the man I'm jealous of and whose death I long for.

FERNANDO. ¡Que sucediese a los ojos   2035
           del Rey y que viese Inés
           que aquel su galán dichoso
           hiciese el toro pedazos
           por libraros!
RODRIGO.   Estoy loco.
           No hay hombre tan desdichado,   2040
           Fernando, de polo a polo.
           ¡Qué de afrentas, qué de penas,
           qué de agravios, qué de enojos,
           qué de injurias, qué de celos,
           qué de agüeros, qué de asombros!   2045
           Alcé los ojos a ver
           a Inés, por ver si piadoso
           mostraba el semblante entonces
           que aungue ingrato, necio adoro;
           y veo que no pudiera   2050
           mirar Nerón riguroso
           desde la torre Tarpeya
           de Roma el incendio, como
           desde el balcón me miraba;
           y que luego, en vergonzoso   2055
           clavel de púrpura fina
           bañado el jazmín del rostro,
           a don Alonso miraba,
           y que por los labios rojos
           pagaba en perlas el gusto   2060
           de ver que a sus pies me postro,
           de la fortuna arrojado,
           y de la suya envidioso.
           Mas ¡vive Dios que la risa,
           primero que la de Apolo   2065
           alegre el Oriente y bañe
           el aire de átomos de oro,
           se le ha de trocar en llanto,
           si hallo al hidalguillo loco
           entre Medina y Olmedo!   2070
FERNANDO. Él sabrá ponerse en cobro.

2049. *que ... adoro*] H; *que como ingrato, y necio adoro* 1641 (a line which is a
syllable too long and defective in sense); *que como un gran necio adoro* R.

FERNANDO.

How horrible that it should have happened before the King's eyes and that Inés should see her lucky young man cut the bull up in order to free you.

RODRIGO.

I'll go mad with rage. In the whole world, Fernando, there's no man so unfortunate as I am. What affronts, what suffering, what offenses, what anger, what insults, what jealousy, what omens, what fright! I raised my eyes to see Inés, to see if compassion showed on that face which, despite its cruelty, I foolishly adore. And I saw that she looked on me from her balcony as sternly as Nero when he watched Rome burning from the tower of Tarpeia.[76] And then, the jasmine white of her cheeks bathed in shameful blushes of exquisite flower pink, she looked at Don Alonso, while her red lips smiled with pleasure[77] to see me prostrate at his feet, cast down by fortune, and envious of his. But, by heaven, I swear that if I find that foolish, insufferable little upstart between Medina and Olmedo, her smile will be changed into tears before the sun's rays brighten the East and bathe the air in atoms of gold.

FERNANDO.

He'll have enough sense to stay out of your way.

RODRIGO. Mal conocéis a los celos.

FERNANDO. ¿Quién sabe que no son monstruos?
    Mas lo que ha de importar mucho
    no se ha de pensar tan poco. *Vanse.* 2075

    Salen el Rey, *el* Condestable *y criados.*

REY. Tarde acabaron las fiestas;
    pero ellas han sido tales,
    que no las he visto iguales.

CONDESTABLE. Dije a Medina que aprestas
    para mañana partir;   2080
    mas tiene tanto deseo
    de que veas el torneo
    con que te quiere servir,
    que me ha pedido, Señor,
    que dos días se detenga 2085
    Vuestra Alteza.

REY.   Cuando venga,
    pienso que será mejor.

CONDESTABLE. Haga este gusto a Medina
    Vuestra Alteza.

REY.   Por vos, sea,
    aunque el Infante desea, 2090
    con tanta prisa camina,
    estas vistas de Toledo
    para el día concertado.

CONDESTABLE. Galán y bizarro ha estado
    el caballero de Olmedo. 2095

REY.   ¡Buenas suertes, condestable!

CONDESTABLE. No sé en él cuál es mayor,
    la ventura o el valor,
    aunque es el valor notable.

REY.   Cualquiera cosa hace bien. 2100

CONDESTABLE. Con razón le favorece
    Vuestra Alteza.

REY.   Él lo merece
    y que vos le honréis también.

  Vanse, y salen Don Alonso *y* Tello, *de noche.*

2075. S.D. Vanse.] H; *Salen* (Enter) 1641.

RODRIGO.
You little know the power of jealousy.

FERNANDO.
Jealousy is surely a terrible monster, as everyone knows. But a thing as important as this should be considered more carefully.

Exeunt.

Enter the King, *the* Lord High Constable, *and their retinue.*

KING.
The festival ended late, but I've never seen one to equal it.

CONSTABLE.
I've told the Medina people that you're preparing to leave tomorrow, but they so much want you to see the tourney planned in your honor that they've asked me to beg Your Highness to stay a day longer.

KING.
I think it would be better to stop on the way back from Toledo.

CONSTABLE.
I beg Your Highness to give this pleasure to Medina.

KING.
For your sake I'll do it, although the Infante[78] is traveling with such haste that he greatly desires this meeting at Toledo to be on the day we had agreed upon.

CONSTABLE.
The knight of Olmedo showed himself to be gallant and magnanimous.

KING.
What fine thrusts he made, Constable!

CONSTABLE.
I don't know which he possesses in higher degree, good luck or courage, though to be sure his courage is exceptional.

KING.
He does everything well.

CONSTABLE.
Your Highness has good cause to favor him.

KING.
He deserves both my favor and yours.   *Exeunt.*

[*Street and exterior view of Don Pedro's house and garden wall.*]
Enter Don Alonso *and* Tello, *dressed for the evening.*[79]

TELLO.   Mucho habemos esperado,
               ya no puedes caminar.   2105
ALONSO.   Deseo, Tello, escusar
               a mis padres el cuidado.
               A cualquier hora es forzoso
               partirme.
TELLO.   Si hablas a Inés,
               ¿qué importa, señor, que estés   2110
               de tus padres cuidadoso?
               Porque os ha de hallar el día
               en esas rejas.
ALONSO.   No hará,
               que el alma me avisará
               como si no fuera mía.   2115
TELLO.   Parece que hablan en ellas
               y que es, en la voz, Leonor.
ALONSO.   Y lo dice el resplandor
               que da el sol a las estrellas.

                    Leonor, *en la reja.*

LEONOR.   ¿Es don Alonso?
ALONSO.   Yo soy.   2120
LEONOR.   Luego mi hermana saldrá,
               porque con mi padre está
               hablando en las fiestas de hoy.
               Tello puede entrar, que quiere
               daros un regalo Inés.   2125
ALONSO.   Entra, Tello.
TELLO.   Si después
               cerraren y no saliere,
               bien puedes partir sin mí,
               que yo te sabré alcanzar.
ALONSO.   ¿Cuándo, Leonor, podré entrar   2130
               con tal libertad aquí?

2129. *alcanzar*] 1641; H, RAE, B all indicate, correctly, Tello's exit here.

TELLO.

We've delayed a long time; it's too late for you to travel now.

ALONSO.

I want to spare my parents worry, Tello. No matter what the hour is, I must make the trip.

TELLO.

If you're going to talk to Inés, master, what sense is there in being concerned about your parents? Dawn is bound to find you still at the iron bars of this garden.

ALONSO.

No, it won't. My heart will warn me of the time as if it belonged to a stranger.

TELLO.

I think I hear someone speaking behind the grating. By the voice, it must be Leonor.

ALONSO.

You're right. The stars shine brighter now in the light reflected from her sun.

[*Enter* Doña] Leonor, *at the grating.*

LEONOR.

Is that Don Alonso?

ALONSO.

It is.

LEONOR.

My sister will be out presently. She's talking with my father now about today's festival. Tello can come in, for Inés wants to give him a present for you.

ALONSO.

Go on in, Tello.

TELLO.

If they shut the house up while I'm inside, you can leave without me; I'll be able to catch up with you.

[*Exit* Tello, *through the door of Don Pedro's house.*]

ALONSO.

Oh Leonor, when will I be able to enter here that freely?

LEONOR.	Pienso que ha de ser muy presto,
	porque mi padre de suerte
	te encarece, que a quererte
	tiene el corazón dispuesto. 2135
	Y porque se case Inés,
	en sabiendo vuestro amor,
	sabrá escoger lo mejor,
	como estimarlo después.

Sale Doña Inés *a la reja.*

INÉS.	¿Con quién hablas?
LEONOR.	Con Rodrigo. 2140
INÉS.	Mientes, que mi dueño es.
ALONSO.	Que soy esclavo de Inés
	al cielo doy por testigo.
INÉS.	No sois sino mi señor.
LEONOR.	Ahora bien, quiéroos dejar, 2145
	que es necedad estorbar,
	sin celos, quien tiene amor.
INÉS.	¿Como estáis?
ALONSO.	Como sin vida.
	Por vivir os vengo a ver.
INÉS.	Bien había menester 2150
	la pena desta partida,
	para templar el contento
	que hoy he tenido de veros
	ejemplo de caballeros
	y de las damas tormento. 2155
	De todas estoy celosa;
	que os alabasen quería,
	y después me arrepentía,
	de perderos temerosa.
	¡Qué de varios pareceres! 2160
	¡Qué de títulos y nombres
	os dio la envidia en los hombres,
	y el amor en las mujeres!
	Mi padre os ha codiciado
	por yerno para Leonor, 2165

2147. *amor*] 1641; H adds here the indication that Leonor leaves the stage.

LEONOR.

Very soon now, I think, because my father extols you so highly
that his heart must be disposed to love you. And when he finds
out about your love, in his desire for Inés to get married, he'll
be able to choose the better suitor and esteem him afterward.

Enter Doña Inés, *at the grating.*

INÉS [*to* Doña Leonor].
Whom were you talking to?
LEONOR.
Rodrigo.
INÉS.
You lie, for it is my dear lord to whom you speak.
ALONSO.
Heaven is my witness that I am Inés's slave.
INÉS.
You are nothing less than my lord and master.
LEONOR.
All right, I'll leave you now; it's foolishness to stand in the way
of lovers, if you're not jealous of them.

[*Exit* Doña Leonor.]

INÉS.
How are you, my love?
ALONSO.
As if I were dead. I come to see you in order to live.
INÉS.
The sorrow of this parting was truly needed to temper the joy
I've had seeing you today the model for all knights and the
torment of all ladies. I'm jealous of all of them, for I wanted
them to praise you, and then I repented of the thought, fearful
of losing you. What a variety of opinions there were! What
names and epithets envy inspired in the men, and love in the
women! My father is greedy to have you as a son-in-law for

<pre>
                    y agradecióle mi amor,
                    aunque celosa, el cuidado;
                       que habéis de ser para mí
                    y así se lo dije yo,
                    aunque con la lengua no,   2170
                    pero con el alma sí.
                       Mas ¡ay! ¿Cómo estoy contenta
                    si os partís?
ALONSO.   Mis padres son
                    la causa.
INÉS.   Tenéis razón;
                    mas dejadme que lo sienta.   2175
ALONSO.   Yo lo siento, y voy a Olmedo,
                    dejando el alma en Medina.
                    No sé cómo parto y quedo;
                    amor la ausencia imagina,
                    los celos, señora, el miedo.   2180
                    Así parto muerto y vivo,
                    que vida y muerte recibo.
                    Mas ¿qué te puedo decir,
                    cuando estoy para partir,
                    puesto ya el pie en el estribo?   2185
                       Ando, señora, estos días,
                    entre tantas asperezas
                    de imaginaciones mías,
                    consolado en mis tristezas
                    y triste en mis alegrías.   2190
                    Tengo, pensando perderte,
                    imaginación tan fuerte,
                    y así en ella vengo y voy,
                    que me parece que estoy
                    con las ansias de la muerte.   2195
                       La envidia de mis contrarios
                    temo tanto, que aunque puedo
                    poner medios necesarios,
                    estoy entre amor y miedo
                    haciendo discursos varios.   2200
                    Ya para siempre me privo
                    de verte, y de suerte vivo,
                    que mi muerte presumiendo,
</pre>

Leonor, and my love was grateful to him for it, though jealousy troubled me, for you are meant for me, and so I told him, though not with my tongue but in my heart. But, alas, how can I be happy if you are leaving?

ALONSO.

It's my parents who are responsible.

INÉS.

You're right in going, but allow me to be sorry for it.

ALONSO.

I'm sorry too, for I'm going to Olmedo but leaving my soul in Medina. I do not know how I both leave and stay at the same time. My love imagines already the pain of absence, while jealousy stirs up my fears. And so I leave both dead and alive, receiving from your hands both death and life. But what more can I say to you, if I am ready to depart, *with one foot already in the stirrup?* I walk these days, my lady, in a harsh wilderness created by my wild fancies, consoled in my sadness and sad in my joy. On the one hand, when I think of losing you, I suffer from such vividly imagined pains, which beset me constantly, that it seems to me *I am possessed by a fearful longing for death.* And, then, the envy of my rivals arouses such fear in me that, even though I might take the necessary steps against them, I am caught between love and fear, arguing with myself interminably. Now and forever I am deprived of seeing you, and I live convinced that I shall die, so that with these words, *my*

parece que estoy diciendo:
«*Señora, aquesta te escribo.*»   2205
Tener de tu esposo el nombre
amor y favor ha sido;
pero es justo que me asombre,
que amado y favorecido
tenga tal tristeza un hombre.   2210
Parto a morir, y te escribo
mi muerte, si ausente vivo,
porque tengo, Inés, por cierto
que si vuelvo será muerto,
pues partir no puedo vivo.   2215
Bien sé que tristeza es;
pero puede tanto en mí,
que me dice, hermosa Inés:
«Si partes muerto de aquí,
¿cómo volverás después?»   2220
Yo parto, y parto a la muerte,
aunque morir no es perderte;
que si el alma no se parte,
¿cómo es posible dejarte,
cuanto más volver a verte?   2225

INÉS.   Pena me has dado y temor
con tus miedos y recelos;
si tus tristezas son celos,
ingrato ha sido tu amor.
Bien entiendo tus razones;   2230
pero tú no has entendido
mi amor.

ALONSO.   Ni tú, que han sido
estas imaginaciones
sólo un ejercicio triste
del alma, que me atormenta,   2235
no celos; que fuera afrenta
del nombre, Inés, que me diste.
De sueños y fantasías,
si bien falsas ilusiones,
han nacido estas razones,   2240
que no de sospechas mías.

                    Leonor sale a la reja.

lady, I must say my last farewell. To bear the name of your husband has been a priceless token of your love and favor. With just cause I am amazed that a man so loved and favored should also feel such sadness. But I depart to die and speak to you now of my death, for even though I should yet survive a while parted from you, I know, Inés, that I will be dead when I return, *for I cannot hope to leave alive.* I know well that melancholy has inspired these words, but it weighs heavy upon me, lovely Inés, and whispers to me, "If you leave here dead, how can you ever return again?" So I leave, and I leave for death, although to die is not to lose you. For if the soul does not depart, how is it possible to leave you, *much less come again to see you?*[80]

INÉS.

You've made me sad and fearful with your own fear and suspicion; if your sadness springs from jealousy, your love shows itself ungrateful. I understand your words well; but you have not understood my love.

ALONSO.

Nor have you understood my words; these fancies are nothing more than a melancholy exercise imposed by my tormented heart, and not by jealousy; to be jealous would offend against the sweet name of husband you gave me, Inés. My words were born not from jealous suspicions but from dreams and fantasies, no doubt all false illusions.

Enter [Doña] Leonor, *at the grating.*

INÉS.	Leonor vuelve. ¿Hay algo?
LEONOR.	Sí.
ALONSO.	¿Es partirme?
LEONOR.	Claro está.
	Mi padre se acuesta ya
	y me preguntó por ti. 2245
INÉS.	Vete, Alonso, vete. Adiós.
	No te quejes, fuerza es.
ALONSO.	¿Cuándo querrá Dios, Inés,
	que estemos juntos los dos?
	Aquí se acabó mi vida, 2250
	que es lo mismo que partirme.
	Tello no sale, o no puede
	acabar de despedirse.
	Voyme, que él me alcanzará.

*Al entrar, una Sombra con una máscara negra y sombrero,
y puesta la mano en el puño de la espada, se le ponga delante.*

ALONSO.	¿Qué es esto? ¿Quién va? De oírme 2255
	no hace caso. ¿Quién es? Hable.
	¡Que un hombre me atemorice,
	no habiendo temido a tantos!
	¿Es don Rodrigo? ¿No dice
	quién es?
SOMBRA.	Don Alonso.
ALONSO.	¿Cómo? 2260
SOMBRA.	Don Alonso.
ALONSO.	No es posible.
	Mas otro será, que yo
	soy don Alonso Manrique.
	Si es invención, ¡meta mano!
	Volvió la espalda. Seguirle, 2265
	desatino me parece.
	¡Oh imaginación terrible!
	Mi sombra debió de ser.

2254. *alcanzará*] 1641; H indicates Inés's exit at this point; M suggests it is more
likely at vs. 2249. The present English translation follows H.
2264. *mano*] 1641; H adds here indication of the *Sombra's* exit.

INÉS.

Leonor is coming back. [*To* Doña Leonor.]   Is something wrong?

LEONOR.

Yes.

ALONSO.

It's time for me to go?

LEONOR.

Indeed.   [*To* Doña Inés.]   Father is going to bed now and has asked for you.

INÉS.

Go, Alonso, go. Goodby. Don't complain; we can do nothing else.

ALONSO.

When may it please God, Inés, for us to be together? Here my life is ended, for parting is the same as dying. Tello isn't leaving, or he hasn't been able to get through his goodbyes. I'm going now; he'll catch up with me.

[*Exeunt* Doña Inés *and* Doña Leonor.]

Enter Shade, *a dark figure with a black mask and a hat on, his hand on his sword hilt; he stands in front of* Don Alonso.

ALONSO.

What's this? Who goes there? —He pays no attention to my voice. —Who is it? Speak. —To think that a man frightens me when I've never trembled before so many others! —Is it Don Rodrigo? Won't you say who you are?

SHADE.

Don Alonso.

ALONSO.

What are you saying?

SHADE.

Don Alonso.

ALONSO.

It's not possible. But it must be another Alonso, for I'm Don Alonso Manrique. —If it's a trick, then draw your sword!

[*Exit* Shade.]

He's turned his back on me. It seems folly to pursue him. Oh, the terrible power of imagination! It must have been my shade.

Mas no, que en forma visible
dijo que era don Alonso.   2270
Todas son cosas que finge
la fuerza de la tristeza,
la imaginación de un triste.
¿Qué me quieres, pensamiento,
que con mi sombra me afliges?   2275
Mira que temer sin causa
es de sujetos humildes.
O embustes de Fabia son,
que pretende persuadirme
porque no me vaya a Olmedo,   2280
sabiendo que es imposible.
Siempre dice que me guarde,
y siempre que no camine
de noche, sin más razón
de que la envidia me sigue.   2285
Pero ya no puede ser
que don Rodrigo me envidie,
pues hoy la vida me debe;
que esta deuda no permite
que un caballero tan noble   2290
en ningún tiempo la olvide.
Antes pienso que ha de ser
para que amistad confirme
desde hoy conmigo en Medina;
que la ingratitud no vive   2295
en buena sangre, que siempre
entre villanos reside.
En fin es la quinta esencia
de cuantas acciones viles
tiene la bajeza humana   2300
pagar mal quien bien recibe.   *Vase.*

Salen Don Rodrigo, Don Fernando, Mendo y Laín.

RODRIGO.   Hoy tendrán fin mis celos y su vida.
FERNANDO.   Finalmente, ¿venís determinado?
RODRIGO.   No habrá consejo que su muerte impida,
              después que la palabra me han quebrado.   2305
              Ya se entendió la devoción fingida,

But no, I saw him and he said he was Don Alonso. These things are all illusions invented by my melancholy, by the imagination of a man beset by sadness. What do you want of me, oh my fancies, to afflict me with my own shade? Only lowborn people are afraid with no reason. Or perhaps it's only a trick of Fabia's, trying to persuade me not to go to Olmedo when she knows that I must. She's always telling me to take care and never to travel by night, only because envy pursues me. But Don Rodrigo can't envy me any longer, for today he owes me his life; and such a debt can never be forgotten by so noble a knight. On the contrary, I think that this debt will make him seal a bond of friendship with me from today on in Medina; for ingratitude is always found in peasant hearts and has no place in the wellborn. In truth, to return evil for good is the quintessence of all vile actions to be found in human baseness.

Exit.

[*The road to Olmedo.*]
Enter Don Rodrigo, Don Fernando, Mendo, *and* Laín.

R O D R I G O .
Today my jealousy and his life will come to an end.
F E R N A N D O .
So finally you are resolved to do this deed?
R O D R I G O .
Nobody's counsel can prevent my killing him since I've learned that they've all broken their word to me. It's clear now what lies behind her feigned devotions; I've learned now that it was

ya supe que era Tello, su criado,
quien la enseñaba aquel latín que ha sido
en cartas de romance traducido.
¡Qué honrada dueña recibió en su casa   2310
don Pedro en Fabia! ¡Oh mísera doncella!
Disculpo tu inocencia, si te abrasa
fuego infernal de los hechizos della.
No sabe, aunque es discreta, lo que pasa,
y así el honor de entrambos atropella.   2315
¡Cuántas casas de nobles caballeros
han infamado hechizos y terceros!
Fabia, que puede trasponer un monte;
Fabia, que puede detener un río
y en los negros ministros de Aqueronte   2320
tiene, como en vasallos, señorío;
Fabia, que deste mar, deste horizonte,
al abrasado clima, al Norte frío
puede llevar un hombre por el aire,
le da liciones. ¿Hay mayor donaire?   2325

FERNANDO. Por la misma razón yo no tratara
de más venganza.
RODRIGO.   ¡Vive Dios, Fernando,
que fuera de los dos bajeza clara!
FERNANDO. No la hay mayor que despreciar amando.
RODRIGO. Si vos podéis, yo no.
MENDO.   Señor, repara   2330
en que vienen los ecos avisando
de que a caballo alguna gente viene.
RODRIGO. Si viene acompañado, miedo tiene.
FERNANDO. No lo creas, que es mozo temerario.
RODRIGO. Todo hombre con silencio esté escondido. 2335
Tú, Mendo, el arcabuz, si es necesario,
tendrás detrás de un árbol prevenido.
FERNANDO. ¡Qué inconstante es el bien, qué loco y vario!
Hoy a vista de un rey salió lucido,
admirado de todos a la plaza,   2340
y ¡ya tan fiera muerte le amenaza!

Escóndanse, y salga Don Alonso.

2319. *río*] H; *risco* (crag) 1641. *Risco* does not rhyme properly with *señorío*.

Alonso's servant Tello who taught her that Latin translated into the good Castilian of love letters. What an honorable duenna Don Pedro took into his house when he received Fabia! Oh miserable girl! I absolve your innocence of wrongdoing if the infernal fire of her spells consumes you. Inés can't know what's going on, even though she is intelligent, and so she tramples heedlessly on her own and her father's honor. How many noble houses have been discredited by witchcraft and go-betweens! Fabia, who can move mountains; Fabia, who can hold back a river's course and who wields sovereign power over her vassals, the dark ministers of Acheron; Fabia, who can carry a man through the air from this sea and this horizon to the burning equator or the frozen North—this is the woman who gives her lessons. Have you ever heard a greater joke?

FERNANDO.

For that very reason I wouldn't seek any further vengeance.

RODRIGO.

By heaven, Fernando, the infamy of them both is clear.

FERNANDO.

It's true there's nothing more vile than to scorn the one who loves you.

RODRIGO.

You may be able to bear the insult, but I cannot.

MENDO.

Master, listen; the echoes give warning that someone is approaching on horseback.

RODRIGO.

If he's brought someone with him, he must be afraid.

FERNANDO.

Don't believe it; he's a reckless lad.

RODRIGO.

All of you men hide silently. You, Mendo, stay behind a tree and keep your harquebus[81] at the ready in case it's needed.

FERNANDO.

How fickle is fortune's favor, how inconstant and changeable! Today, admired by everyone in the plaza, he shone splendidly before the eyes of a king, and only a little while after, so cruel a death threatens him!

They hide, and Don Alonso *enters.*

ALONSO.   Lo que jamás he tenido,
                 que es algún recelo o miedo,
                 llevo caminando a Olmedo.
                 Pero tristezas han sido.   2345
                 Del agua el manso rüido
                 y el ligero movimiento
                 destas ramas, con el viento,
                 mi tristeza aumentan más.
                 Yo camino, y vuelve atrás   2350
                 mi confuso pensamiento.
                 De mis padres el amor
                 y la obediencia me lleva,
                 aunque esta es pequeña prueba
                 del alma de mi valor.   2355
                 Conozco que fue rigor
                 el dejar tan presto a Inés.
                 ¡Qué escuridad! Todo es
                 horror, hasta que el Aurora   *Toca.*
                 en las alfombras de Flora   2360
                 ponga los dorados pies.
                 Allí cantan. ¿Quién será?
                 Mas será algún labrador
                 que camina a su labor.
                 Lejos parece que está,   2365
                 pero acercándose va.
                 Pues ¡cómo! Lleva instrumento,
                 y no es rústico el acento,
                 sino sonoro y süave.
                 ¡Qué mal la música sabe,   2370
                 si está triste el pensamiento!

Canten desde lejos en el vestuario, y véngase acercando la voz,
                 como que camina.

                 Que de noche le mataron
                 al caballero,
                 la gala de Medina,
                 la flor de Olmedo.   2375

2342. *tenido*] H; *temido* (feared) 1641.
2359. S.D. *Toca*] 1641; H omits; R inserts *Tocan* after vs. 2362.

ALONSO.

Misgivings and fear, things I've never suffered, beset me now on this journey to Olmedo. But it's only my melancholy. The gentle sound of the water and the light movement of the branches as the wind passes through them add to my sadness. I go forward, while my confused thoughts turn backward. Love for my parents and the obedience I owe them carry me onward, though this journey by night is a puny test of my courage. I know that it was cruel to leave Inés so soon— What impenetrable darkness! The night is full of horror until Aurora sets her golden feet on Flora's carpets. (*Music is heard.*) Someone's singing over there. Who can it be? It must be some peasant going out to his fields. He seems far off, but he's coming closer. But how can it be? He has an instrument with him, and his accents are not rustic but sonorous and soft. How ill does music sound when one's thoughts are melancholy!

*Singing is heard distantly from offstage, but the voice comes
ever closer.*

[VOICE, *off.*]

> *So by night they killed him,*
> *the noble knight,*
> *glory of Medina,*
> *flower of Olmedo.*

ALONSO.	¡Cielos! ¿Qué estoy escuchando?
	Si es que avisos vuestros son,
	ya que estoy en la ocasión,
	¿de qué me estáis informando?
	Volver atrás, ¿cómo puedo? 2380
	Invención de Fabia es,
	que quiere, a ruego de Inés,
	hacer que no vaya a Olmedo.
LA VOZ.	*Sombras le avisaron*
	que no saliese, 2385
	y le aconsejaron
	que no se fuese
	el caballero,
	la gala de Medina,
	la flor de Olmedo. 2390
ALONSO.	¡Hola, buen hombre, el que canta!
LABRADOR.	¿Quién me llama?
ALONSO.	Un hombre soy
	que va perdido.
LABRADOR.	Ya voy.

Sale un Labrador.

	Veisme aquí.
ALONSO.	Todo me espanta.
	¿Dónde vas?
LABRADOR.	A mi labor. 2395
ALONSO.	¿Quién esa canción te ha dado,
	que tristemente has cantado?
LABRADOR.	Allá en Medina, señor.
ALONSO.	A mí me suelen llamar
	el caballero de Olmedo, 2400
	y yo estoy vivo.
LABRADOR.	No puedo
	deciros deste cantar
	más historias ni ocasión,
	de que a una Fabia la oí.
	Si os importa, yo cumplí 2405
	con deciros la canción.
	Volved atrás, no paséis
	deste arroyo.

ALONSO.

Heaven protect me! What do I hear? If these warnings come from heaven, what are they trying to tell me now that I am here on the road? That I should turn back? But how can I? It's all a trick of Fabia's; Inés has begged her to keep me from going to Olmedo.

VOICE [*off*].

> *Shades have warned him*
> *not to set out,*
> *they counseled him*
> *he should not go,*
> *the noble knight,*
> *glory of Medina,*
> *flower of Olmedo.*

ALONSO.

Hallo there, good fellow, you who are singing!

PEASANT [*off*].

Who calls me?

ALONSO.

I'm a man who's lost his way.

PEASANT [*off*].

I'm coming.

Enter a Peasant.

Here I am.

ALONSO [*aside*].

Everything frightens me. —Where are you going?

PEASANT.

Out to work.

ALONSO.

Who gave you that song you've sung so mournfully?

PEASANT.

Somebody in Medina, sir.

ALONSO.

People are accustomed to call me the knight from Olmedo, and I'm alive.

PEASANT.

I can't tell you anything more about that song except that I heard it from a woman called Fabia. If it concerns you, I can do no more; I've done my job by singing the song to you. Turn back; don't pass beyond this stream.

ALONSO.	En mi nobleza,
	fuera ese temor bajeza.
LABRADOR.	¡Muy necio valor tenéis! 2410
	Volved, volved a Medina.
ALONSO.	Ven tú conmigo.
LABRADOR.	No puedo.
ALONSO.	¡Qué de sombras finge el miedo!
	¡Qué de engaños imagina!
	Oye, escucha. ¿Dónde fue, 2415
	que apenas sus pasos siento?
	¡Ah, labrador! Oye, aguarda.
	«Aguarda», responde el eco.
	¡Muerto yo! Pero es canción
	que por algún hombre hicieron 2420
	de Olmedo, y los de Medina
	en este camino han muerto.
	A la mitad dél estoy:
	¿qué han de decir si me vuelvo?
	Gente viene. No me pesa; 2425
	si allá van, iré con ellos.

Salgan Don Rodrigo *y* Don Fernando *y su gente.*

RODRIGO.	¿Quién va?
ALONSO.	Un hombre. ¿No me ven?
FERNANDO.	Deténgase.
ALONSO.	Caballeros,
	si acaso necesidad
	los fuerza a pasos como éstos, 2430
	desde aquí a mi casa hay poco.
	No habré menester dineros,
	que de día y en la calle
	se los doy a cuantos veo
	que me hacen honra en pedirlos. 2435
RODRIGO.	Quítese las armas luego.
ALONSO.	¿Para qúe?
RODRIGO.	Para rendillas.

2412. *puedo*] 1641; H inserts here indication of the *Labrador*'s exit.

ALONSO.

To admit fear and turn back would be unworthy of my nobility.

PEASANT.

What foolish courage! Turn back, turn back to Medina.

ALONSO.

You come with me.

PEASANT.

I can't.

[*Exit the* Peasant.]

ALONSO.

What phantoms fear invents! What illusions it imagines!—Listen to me, man, hear me. — But where did he go? I can scarcely hear his footsteps now. —Oh, plowman! Listen, wait. —"Wait," answers the echo. To think, he says I'm dead! But it's surely a song they made up about some fellow from Olmedo murdered by men from Medina on this very road. And now I'm at the midpoint of it. What will they say of me if I turn back? I hear people coming. And I'm not sorry; if they're going my way, I'll go with them.

Enter Don Rodrigo *and* Don Fernando *and their men.*

RODRIGO.

Who goes there?

ALONSO.

A man. Don't you see me?

FERNANDO.

Stop.

ALONSO.

Gentlemen, if perhaps poverty forces you to this extreme, take my money.[82] It's only a short way from here to my house, and I'll have no need of it. By day and in the street I give money to all who do me the honor of asking for it.

RODRIGO.

Take off your weapons at once.

ALONSO.

What for?

RODRIGO.

To surrender them.

ALONSO. ¿Saben quién soy?

FERNANDO.   El de Olmedo,
el matador de los toros,
que viene arrogante y necio   2440
a afrentar los de Medina;
el que deshonra a don Pedro
con alcagüetes infames.

ALONSO.   Si fuérades a lo menos
nobles vosotros, allá,   2445
pues tuvistes tanto tiempo,
me hablárades, y no agora,
que solo a mi case vuelvo.
Allá en las rejas, adonde
dejastes la capa huyendo,   2450
fuera bien, y no en cuadrilla
a media noche, soberbios.
Pero confieso, villanos,
que la estimación os debo,
que aun siendo tantos, sois pocos.   2455
                              Riñan.

RODRIGO.   Yo vengo a matar, no vengo
a desafíos; que entonces
te matara cuerpo a cuerpo.
Tírale.   *Disparen dentro.*

ALONSO.   Traidores sois;
pero sin armas de fuego   2460
no pudiérades matarme.
¡Jesús!

FERNANDO.   ¡Bien lo has hecho, Mendo!

ALONSO.   ¡Qué poco crédito di
a los avisos del cielo!
Valor propio me ha engañado,   2465
y muerto envidias y celos.
¡Ay de mí! ¿Qué haré en un campo
tan solo?

                    Sale Tello.

2462. *Mendo*] 1641; H adds here indication that Rodrigo, Fernando, and their men leave the stage.
2468. *tan solo*] H; 1641 puts Tello's entrance before these words.

ALONSO.

Do you know who I am?

FERNANDO.

The fellow from Olmedo, the slayer of bulls, who comes arrogantly and foolishly to affront the citizens of Medina; you're the man who dishonors Don Pedro with infamous go-betweens.

ALONSO.

If you yourselves were noble and honorable, you would have spoken to me there, for you had sufficient time, and not now, when I'm going home alone. There, by the garden window, where you left your cape when you fled, it would have been well, and not in a gang at midnight and so haughtily. But I confess, base villains, that I owe you some thanks for your behavior, because even if you are many in numbers, you are few in valor.   *They fight.*

RODRIGO.

I've come to kill you, not to fight a duel; if I'd chosen a duel, I would have killed you man to man. Shoot him.

Shots offstage.

ALONSO.

You are treacherous knaves, but without firearms you could not have killed me! Oh, sweet Christ!

FERNANDO.

You hit your mark well, Mendo!

[*Exeunt* Don Rodrigo, Don Fernando, *and their men.*]

ALONSO.

How little credit I gave to warnings from heaven! Trust in my own valor has deceived me, and envy and jealousy have killed me. Heaven pity me! What can I do alone in this field?

Enter Tello.

TELLO.	Pena me dieron
	estos hombres que a caballo
	van hacia Medina huyendo.
	Si a don Alonso habían visto
	pregunté; no respondieron.
	¡Mala señal! Voy temblando.
ALONSO.	¡Dios mío, piedad! ¡Yo muero!
	Vos sabéis que fue mi amor
	dirigido a casamiento.
	¡Ay, Inés!
TELLO.	De lastimosas
	quejas siento tristes ecos.
	Hacia aquella parte suenan.
	No está del camino lejos
	quien las da. No me ha quedado
	sangre; pienso que el sombrero
	puede tenerse en el aire
	solo en cualquiera cabello.
	¡Ah, hidalgo!
ALONSO.	¿Quién es?
TELLO.	¡Ay, Dios!
	¿Por qué dudo lo que veo?
	¡Es mi señor don Alonso!
ALONSO.	Seas bien venido, Tello.
TELLO.	¿Cómo, señor, si he tardado?
	¿Cómo, si a mirarte llego
	hecho una fiera de sangre?
	¡Traidores, villanos, perros,
	volved, volved a matarme,
	pues habéis, infames, muerto
	el más noble, el más valiente,
	el más galán caballero
	que ciñó espada en Castilla!
ALONSO.	Tello, Tello, ya no es tiempo
	más que de tratar del alma.
	Ponme en tu caballo presto
	y llévame a ver mis padres.

Line numbers: 2470, 2475, 2480, 2485, 2490, 2495, 2500

2491. *una fiera*] 1641; *un piélago* (sea) H.

TELLO.

Those men on horseback fleeing toward Medina troubled me. I asked them if they had seen Don Alonso, and they didn't answer. A bad sign! I'm trembling with fear.

ALONSO.

Oh my God, mercy! I am dying! Thou knowest that my love was bent on marriage. Oh, Inés!

TELLO.

I hear the sad echoes of piteous moans. They seem to come from over there. Whoever it is is not far from the road. The blood has all left my veins; I think that any hair on my head could hold my hat up all by itself. Hallo there, sir!

ALONSO.

Who is it?

TELLO.

Oh, my God! Why do I doubt what I see? It's my master Don Alonso!

ALONSO.

You are well come, Tello.

TELLO.

How can that be, master, if I've come too late? When I see you turned into a bleeding animal? Traitors, villains, dogs, come back, come back and kill me, for you have, oh shameless men, slain the noblest, the bravest, the most gallant knight who ever girded on his sword in all Castile!

ALONSO.

Tello, Tello, there's no time now but to attend to my soul. Put me on your horse quickly and take me to see my parents.

TELLO.	¡Qué buenas nuevas les llevo
	de las fiestas de Medina!
	¿Qué dirá aquel noble viejo?
	¿Qué hará tu madre y tu patria? 2505
	¡Venganza, piadosos cielos!

Salen Don Pedro, Doña Inés, Doña Leonor, Fabia *y* Ana.

INÉS.	¿Tantas mercedes ha hecho?
PEDRO.	Hoy mostró con su real
	mano, heroica y liberal,
	la grandeza de su pecho. 2510
	Medina está agradecida,
	y, por la que he recibido,
	a besarla os he traído.
LEONOR.	¿Previene ya su partida?
PEDRO.	Sí, Leonor, por el Infante, 2515
	que aguarda al Rey en Toledo.
	En fin, obligado quedo;
	que por merced semejante,
	más por vosotras lo estoy,
	pues ha de ser vuestro aumento. 2520
LEONOR.	Con razón estás contento.
PEDRO.	Alcaide de Burgos soy.
	Besad la mano a Su Alteza.
INÉS.	¿Ha de haber ausencia, Fabia?
FABIA.	Más la fortuna te agravia. 2525
INÉS.	No en vano tanta tristeza
	he tenido desde ayer.
FABIA.	Yo pienso que mayor daño
	te espera, si no me engaño,
	como suele suceder, 2530
	que en las cosas por venir
	no puede haber cierta ciencia.
INÉS.	¿Qué mayor mal que la ausencia,
	pues es mayor que morir?

TELLO.

What good news I bring them from the festival at Medina! What will that noble old man say? What will your mother and your country do? Vengeance, oh merciful heavens!   [*Exeunt.*]

[*A room in the King's residence in Medina.*]
Enter Don Pedro, Doña Inés, Doña Leonor, Fabia, *and Ana.*

INÉS.

The King has granted so many favors then?

PEDRO.

Today his royal hand showed the greatness of his heart in its strength and liberality. All Medina is grateful to him, and I've brought you girls to kiss his hand for the favor I have received.

LEONOR.

Is he preparing to leave already?

PEDRO.

Yes, Leonor, in order to meet the Infante,[8][3] who awaits the King in Toledo. In short, I'm deeply obliged to him, and more for your sakes than for mine, for such a gift will serve for the increase of your estate.

LEONOR.

You have reason to be pleased.

PEDRO.

He's made me Warden of Burgos. For that you must kiss His Highness's hand.

INÉS [*aside to* Fabia].

Must we be separated, Fabia?

FABIA.

Fortune will injure you still more.

INÉS.

There was a reason, then, for such sadness as has possessed me since yesterday.

FABIA.

I fear that greater harm awaits you, if I'm not wrong, as frequently happens, for there can be no certain knowledge about events to come.

INÉS.

What greater ill than absence is there, for it is greater than death?

PEDRO.   Ya, Inés, ¿qué mayores bienes   2535
                pudiera yo desear,
                si tú quisieras dejar
                el propósito que tienes?
                No porque yo te hago fuerza,
                pero quisiera casarte.   2540
INÉS.   Pues tu obediencia no es parte
                que mi propósito tuerza.
                Me admiro de que no entiendas
                la ocasión.
PEDRO.   Yo no la sé.
LEONOR.   Pues yo por ti la diré,   2545
                Inés, como no te ofendas.
                No la casas a su gusto.
                ¡Mira qué presto!
PEDRO.   Mi amor
                se queja de tu rigor,
                porque, a saber tu disgusto,   2550
                no lo hubiera imaginado.
LEONOR.   Tiene inclinación Inés
                a un caballero, después
                que el Rey de una cruz le ha honrado;
                que esto es deseo de honor,   2555
                y no poca honestidad.
PEDRO.   Pues si él tiene calidad
                y tú le tienes amor,
                ¿quién ha de haber que replique?
                Cásate en buen hora, Inés.   2560
                Pero ¿no sabré quién es?
LEONOR.   Es don Alonso Manrique.
PEDRO.   Albricias hubiera dado.
                ¿El de Olmedo?
LEONOR.   Sí, señor.
PEDRO.   Es hombre de gran valor,   2565
                y desde agora me agrado
                de tan discreta elección;
                que si el hábito rehusaba,
                era porque imaginaba
                diferente vocación.   2570
                Habla, Inés, no estés ansí.

PEDRO.

And now, Inés, what greater good could I desire, if you would only abandon your resolve? It's not that I wish to force your will, but I would like to see you married.

INÉS.

Obedience to you cannot shake my resolve. I marvel that you do not understand my reasons.

PEDRO.

I don't know what they are.

LEONOR.

Well, I'll explain them for you, Inés, if you won't take offence. You, sir, are not marrying her to a man she likes. See how quickly it is said!

PEDRO.

My father's heart protests you've treated me unfairly. If I had known of your displeasure, I would never have arranged such a marriage.

LEONOR.

Inés gave her heart to a certain knight after the King honored him with the cross of Alcántara;[84] such feelings reveal her regard for honor, as well as an unusual sense of propriety.

PEDRO.

Well, if he is a man of quality and you are in love with him, who's going to cross your will? Marry him and be happy, Inés. But am I not to know who he is?

LEONOR.

He is Don Alonso Manrique.

PEDRO.

If you'd asked me, I would have given you a reward for such good news. Do you mean the knight from Olmedo?

LEONOR.

Yes, sir.

PEDRO.

He is a man of great courage, and I'm pleased by the discretion of your choice; for if I didn't approve your nun's habit, it was because I thought you better fitted for another vocation. Say something, Inés. Don't be like that.

INÉS.	Señor, Leonor se adelanta;
	que la inclinación no es tanta
	como ella te ha dicho aquí.
PEDRO.	Yo no quiero examinarte, 2575
	sino estar con mucho gusto
	de pensamiento tan justo
	y de que quieras casarte.
	Desde agora es tu marido;
	que me tendré por honrado 2580
	de un yerno tan estimado,
	tan rico y tan bien nacido.
INÉS.	Beso mil veces tus pies.
	Loca de contento estoy,
	Fabia.
FABIA.	El parabién te doy, 2585
	si no es pésame después.
LEONOR.	El Rey.
PEDRO.	Llegad a besar
	su mano.
INÉS.	¡Qué alegre llego!

Salen el Rey, *el* Condestable *y gente, y* Don Rodrigo *y*
Don Fernando.

PEDRO.	Dé Vuestra Alteza los pies,
	por la merced que me ha hecho 2590
	del alcaidía de Burgos,
	a mí y a mis hijas.
REY.	Tengo
	bastante satisfación
	de vuestro valor, don Pedro,
	y de que me habéis servido. 2595
PEDRO.	Por lo menos lo deseo.
REY.	¿Sois casadas?
INÉS.	No, señor.
REY.	¿Vuestro nombre?
INÉS.	Inés.

INÉS.

Sir, Leonor has been too forward; my feeling for him is not so great as she has said here.

PEDRO.

I've no desire to examine your conscience; I only want to express my pleasure at this fine choice and your desire to get married. From this moment, he is your husband, for I'll consider it an honor to have a son-in-law so esteemed, so rich, and so wellborn.

INÉS.

I kiss your feet a thousand times. [*Aside to* Fabia.]   Fabia, I'm mad with joy.

FABIA.

I'll give you my congratulations now, hoping they don't turn into condolences later.

LEONOR.

The King is coming.

PEDRO.

You girls go up to kiss his hand.

INÉS.

How happily I go!

Enter the King, *the* Lord High Constable, *their retinue, and* Don Rodrigo *and* Don Fernando.

PEDRO.

Let me kiss Your Highness's feet for the gift you've made me and my daughters of the Wardenship of Burgos.

KING.

I am well satisfied with your valor, Don Pedro, and your loyal service.

PEDRO.

At least that has been my desire.

KING.

Are you ladies married?

INÉS.

No, Sire.

KING.

What's your name?

INÉS.

Inés.

REY.   ¿Y el vuestro?
LEONOR.   Leonor.
CONDESTABLE.   Don Pedro merece
        tener dos gallardos yernos,   2600
        que están presentes, señor,
        y que yo os pido por ellos
        los caséis de vuestra mano.
REY.   ¿Quién son?
RODRIGO.   Yo, señor, pretendo,
        con vuestra licencia, a Inés.   2605
FERNANDO.   Y yo a su hermana le ofrezco
        la mano y la voluntad.
REY.   En gallardos caballeros
        emplearéis vuestras dos hijas,
        don Pedro.
PEDRO.   Señor, no puedo   2610
        dar a Inés a don Rodrigo,
        porque casada la tengo
        con don Alonso Manrique,
        el caballero de Olmedo,
        a quien hicistes merced   2615
        de un hábito.
REY.   Yo os prometo
        que la primera encomienda
        sea suya...
RODRIGO.   ¡Estraño suceso!
FERNANDO.   Ten prudencia.
REY.   Porque es hombre
        de grandes merecimientos.   2620

                Sale Tello.

TELLO.   Dejadme entrar.
CONDESTABLE.   ¿Quién da voces?
CRIADO.   Con la guarda un escudero
        que quiere hablarte.

2621-2623. *¿Quién . . . hablarte*] the question is assigned by 1641 to *Gente* (people); H assigns *¿Quién da voces?* to *Rey* and the response to the *Condestable*.

KING.

And yours?

LEONOR.

Leonor.

CONSTABLE.

Sire, Don Pedro deserves to have two gallant young men who are here present as his sons-in-law, and that I should ask in their behalf that Your Highness sponsor the marriage.

KING.

Who are they?

RODRIGO.

With your permission, Sire, I am a suitor for the hand of Inés.

FERNANDO.

And I offer her sister my hand and my heart.

KING.

You will be marrying your two daughters to gallant knights, Don Pedro.

PEDRO.

Sire, I cannot give Inés to Don Rodrigo, for I've affianced her already to Don Alonso Manrique, the knight from Olmedo, whom you have favored with a habit.

KING.

I promise you that the first fief of his order that falls vacant will go to him—

RODRIGO [*aside to* Don Fernando].

What a strange turn of events!

FERNANDO [*aside to* Don Rodrigo].

Be cautious.

KING.

—because he is a man of great merit.

Enter Tello.

TELLO [*to a guard*].

Let me go in.

CONSTABLE.

Who's making all that noise?

SERVANT.

There's a squire here arguing with the guards who wants to speak to you.

REY.	Dejadle.
CONDESTABLE.	Viene llorando y pidiendo
	justicia.
REY.	Hacerla es mi oficio.

Eso significa el cetro.

TELLO. Invictísimo don Juan,
que del castellano reino,
a pesar de tanta envidia,
gozas el dichoso imperio:
con un caballero anciano
vine a Medina, pidiendo
justicia de dos traidores;
pero el doloroso exceso
en tus puertas le ha dejado,
si no desmayado, muerto.
Con esto yo, que le sirvo,
rompí con atrevimiento
tus guardas y tus oídos:
oye, pues te puso el cielo
la vara de su justicia
en tu libre entendimiento,
para castigar los malos
y para premiar los buenos.
La noche de aquellas fiestas
que a la Cruz de Mayo hicieron
caballeros de Medina,
para que fuese tan cierto
que donde hay cruz hay pasión,
por dar a sus padres viejos
contento de verle libre
de los toros, menos fieros
que fueron sus enemigos,
partió de Medina a Olmedo
don Alonso, mi señor,
aquel ilustre mancebo
que mereció tu alabanza,
que es raro encarecimiento.
Quedéme en Medina yo,
como a mi cargo estuvieron

2625

2630

2635

2640

2645

2650

2655

2660

KING.

Let him come forward.

CONSTABLE.

He is weeping and begging for justice.

KING.

To administer justice is my principal task. That is what my scepter signifies.

TELLO.

Oh, invincible Don Juan, you who enjoy, despite so many envious rivals,[85] fortunate sovereignty over the kingdom of Castile, I have come to Medina with a noble old man to plead for justice against two traitors. But his extreme grief has left him fainting, if not dead, at your doors, so that I, who serve him, have dared to burst in past your guards and assail your royal ears: hear then, for heaven has given its staff of justice into the keeping of your clear intelligence in order to punish the evildoer and reward the good. On the night of the festival celebrated by the knights of Medina in honor of the May Cross—so that it should indeed be true that where there is a cross, there is passion also—my master Don Alonso, that illustrious youth who merited your praise, the best testimony to his worth, set out from Medina to Olmedo to give his aged parents the happiness of seeing him free from the bulls, less cruel than his human enemies. I stayed in Medina to take care of the horses and their

los jaeces y caballos,
para tener cuenta dellos.
Ya la destocada noche,
de los dos polos en medio,
daba a la traición espada,   2665
mano al hurto, pies al miedo,
cuando partí de Medina;
y al pasar un arroyuelo,
puente y señal del camino,
veo seis hombres corriendo   2670
hacia Medina, turbados
y, aunque juntos, descompuestos.
La luna, que salió tarde,
menguado el rostro sangriento,
me dio a conocer los dos;   2675
que tal vez alumbra el cielo
con las hachas de sus luces
el más escuro silencio,
para que vean los hombres
de las maldades los dueños,   2680
porque a los ojos divinos
no hubiese humanos secretos.
Paso adelante, ¡ay de mí!,
y envuelto en su sangre veo
a don Alonso espirando.   2685
Aquí, gran señor, no puedo
ni hacer resistencia al llanto,
ni decir el sentimiento.
En el caballo le puse
tan animoso, que creo   2690
que pensaban sus contrarios
que no le dejaban muerto.
A Olmedo llegó con vida,
cuanto fue bastante, ¡ay cielo!,
para oír la bendición   2695
de dos miserables viejos,
que enjugaban las heridas
con lágrimas y con besos.

2663. *destocada*] 1641; H substitutes *encapotada* (hooded), for no discernible
reason.

trappings, which was my job. When I left Medina, the wild disheveled night, midway in its course from pole to pole, was already providing treachery with a sword, robbery with hands, and fear with feet. As I passed a little stream which crosses and marks that road, I saw six men running toward Medina in confusion and, though together, in disorder. The moon, which rose late, its bloody face in the waning phase, helped me to recognize two of them; for sometimes heaven lights the deepest and most silent darkness with its torches so men may see the authors of evil deeds, and mortal man should have no secrets hidden from divine eyes. I continued onward, oh alas, and saw Don Alonso dying in a pool of his own blood. Here, oh my lord, I cannot hold back the tears or give tongue to my sorrow. I put him on my horse, and he rode off with such spirit that I think his enemies feared they had not left him dead. He reached Olmedo with enough life left, oh merciful heaven, to hear a blessing from his father and mother, those two wretched old people who cleansed his wounds with tears and kisses. He

	Cubrió de luto su casa	
	y su patria, cuyo entierro	2700
	será el del fénix, Señor,	
	después de muerto viviendo	
	en las lenguas de la fama,	
	a quien conocen respeto	
	la mudanza de los hombres	2705
	y los olvidos del tiempo.	
REY.	¡Estraño caso!	
INÉS.	¡Ay de mí!	
PEDRO.	Guarda lágrimas y estremos,	
	Inés, para nuestra casa.	
INÉS.	Lo que de burlas te dije,	2710
	señor, de veras te ruego.	
	Y a vos, generoso Rey,	
	desos viles caballeros	
	os pido justicia.	
REY.	Dime,	
	pues pudiste conocerlos,	2715
	¿Quién son esos dos traidores?	
	¿Dónde están? Que ¡vive el cielo	
	de no me partir de aquí	
	hasta que los deje presos!	
TELLO.	Presentes están, Señor:	2720
	don Rodrigo es el primero,	
	y don Fernando el segundo.	
CONDESTABLE.	El delito es manifiesto,	
	su turbación lo confiesa.	
RODRIGO.	Señor, escucha...	
REY.	Prendedlos,	2725
	y en un teatro mañana	
	cortad sus infames cuellos:	
	fin de la trágica historia	
	del *Caballero de Olmedo*.	

FIN DE LA COMEDIA

DEL

CABALLERO DE OLMEDO

2709-2710. *Inés ... dije*] 1641; between these two verses at least one line is probably missing, as is indicated by the break in the pattern of assonance.
2713. *desos*] H; *destos* (of these) 1641.

covered his family and his country with mourning, and his burial will be like that of the phoenix, Sire, for he shall live after death on the tongue of fame, to which even the fickleness of men and the oblivion of passing time pay homage.

KING.

A strange affair!

INÉS.

Ah, such sorrow!

PEDRO.

Keep your tears and lamentations until we get home, Inés.[86]

INÉS.

What I said to you in jest, my lord, I now beg you in all seriousness: I wish to become a nun. And from you, oh generous King, I beg for justice against those vile men.

KING.

Tell me, Tello, since you were able to recognize them, who are those two traitors? Where are they? For, by heaven, I swear that I shall not depart from here until they are imprisoned!

TELLO.

They're right here, Sire: Don Rodrigo is one, and Don Fernando is the other.

CONSTABLE.

Their crime is clear, and their confusion bears witness to it.

RODRIGO.

Sire, hear me—

KING.

Seize them, and cut off their infamous necks on the scaffold tomorrow: so ends the tragic history of *The Knight of Olmedo*.

End of the play of *The Knight of Olmedo*.

NOTES TO THE TRANSLATION

1. *when . . . alike*] translation of *con poca diferencia* (literally, "with little difference"); M interprets the phrase as "with little delay," which makes excellent sense in the context; but, though one meaning of the verb *diferir* is "to delay," the noun *diferencia* does not seem ever to have been so used (DA).

2. *Oh love . . . incomplete*] a remarkably compact synthesis of Neoplatonic doctrine with regard to the psychology and physiology of falling in love, with emphasis also on the Aristotelian concepts of matter (the feminine principle), form (the masculine principle), and the complete animal expressed in the *Physica* and *De generatione animalium*. When Alonso says "This love of mine . . . issued from a pair of eyes," the audience is expected to recognize the Neoplatonic optics of love, as explained by Marsilio Ficino and others: when Alonso's eyes fell on his lady for the first time, her vital spirits—a thin vapor distilled by the heart's heat from the purest part of the blood—flowed forth from her body through the eyes as rays of light, passed through his eyes, and sped directly to his soul, where they lit up the image of beauty born within it, and to his heart, where they kindled the fires of his own vital spirits. Already deeply in love, Alonso justifies the passion, still in Neoplatonic terms, as the creative and preservative force in the universe and reminds Cupid that complete love—and the complete offspring to be expected from it—can exist only if he has also shot a golden arrow at the lady rather than the leaden shaft which induces hatred. Typically Neoplatonic also is Inés's later assertion that the perfect mutual love between her and Alonso was foreordained through the influence of the stars and planets ascendant at the time of their birth (vss. 215-228). Indeed there is scarcely a passage dealing with love throughout the play which does not have a close analogue in Ficino's *Commentary on Plato's "Symposium"* and Leone Ebreo's *The Philosophy of Love*.

3. *fair . . . Medina*] Medina del Campo is situated in the north of Spain, some twenty-one miles south of Valladolid. Instituted in the fourteenth century, the famous Medina fair, held in the spring and fall each year, had reached its apogee by the mid-fifteenth century. It was the major wool and money market for all Spain, the greatest market for luxuries—satins, brocades, jewelry, spices, silver—in all Europe, attracting merchants from Ireland, Genoa, Flanders, Florence, etc. In the late sixteenth century, however, the Medina fair suffered a financial crisis, and by the time of composition of this play, the bustle, wealth, and splendor which had characterized it were only a vivid memory.

4. *Bright . . . obvious*] an image based on the practice of smearing sticky birdlime (*liga*) on branches or twigs, thus preventing small birds from flying, so that they might be caught in nets. Garcilaso's *Second Eclogue* describes at length this and other methods of catching birds (vss. 200 ff.). The image of the lady's hair as a net which imprisons the lover's heart is a commonplace of

the Petrarchan poetic tradition. Again, Garcilaso supplies an example, in his *Fourth Canzone*, vss 101-102: "De los cabellos de oro fue tejida/ la red que fabricó mi sentimiento" ("The net which my passion created was woven from her golden hair").

5. *Her . . . cuffs*] These lines compress the more extended image and puns of *Las manos . . . esquinas*. The *valona* was an elegant type of Vandyke collar usually trimmed with lace which hung in points (*esquinas*) over the shoulders, back, and chest; the word here appears to refer to the similar lacy cuffs worn by Inés. Two untranslatable puns are involved: her delicate white wrists (*muñecas*), set off by the pointed (*esquinadas*) cuffs are likened to the paper or cardboard dolls (*muñecas de papel*) sold, as R suggests, in shops on the corners (*esquinas*) of plazas. A passage from *Don Quijote*, II:70 (published 1615), may serve to make the visual image clearer: certain playful devils are described as wearing "Walloon collars trimmed with Flemish bonelace, with ruffles of the same material that served them as cuffs and with four inches of their arms sticking out in order to make their hands . . . appear longer than they were" (trans. Samuel Putnam [New York: Viking Press, 1949]). Needless to say, the articles of dress and styles mentioned here and elsewhere are those of Lope's own day and not of the fifteenth century.

6. *Her . . . town*] Army captains were empowered to recruit their own troops; the regiment's drummer noisily beat his drum in towns along the captain's route to announce each new recruiting drive. *Caja* means drum and also, probably, as R suggests, the box of jam or sweets frequently offered as refreshment in this period.

7. *skirt . . . tongue*] The *basquiña*, or full skirt, is related in sound to *vasco, vascuence*, the name of the Basque language, thus providing in Spanish a sharper punning contrast with the "French" petticoats than can be achieved in English.

8. *slippers . . . straps*] The slippers (*chinelas*) were a high-heeled shoe with no covering for the back of the heel; the straps (*virillas*), frequently of silver or gold, helped bind the sole to the top of the slipper.

9. *asp*] Inés's beauty is as deadly in its effects as the asp's bite; also, she is deaf, like the asp or adder, to the entreaties of her admirers (cf. Psalm 58:3-5, where the poison of the wicked is likened to the poison of a serpent: "They are like the deaf adder that stoppeth her ear; which will not hearken to the voice of charmers . . .").

10. *Yesterday . . . lightly*] This portion of the speech (from "Yesterday afternoon," above) renders the ballad published separately, with slight variants, in Pedro Arias Pérez's anthology of poems published in Madrid in 1621. See Introduction, p. xi.

11. *Olmedo*] a town some thirteen miles to the east of Medina del Campo.

12. *If . . . water*] Inés is likened both to the unicorn, because of the similar purifying powers of the animal's white horn and her white fingers, and the serpent-like basilisk, because her gaze and that of the basilisk are both fatal in their effects. C's definition of these two mythical beasts mentions these magical powers.

13. *knight's cross*] Spanish *encomienda*; R prefers to interpret as "protection"; but the word is also used to mean the cross of his military order embroidered on a knight's cape or habit. I have preferred the visual image.

14. *love ... stars*] See above, note 2.

15. *pure ... Catherine*] C observes that the name, derived from Greek χαθαρος, means "pure"; Fabia's words are meant to praise the purity and modesty of Inés's mother.

16. *camphor and sublimate*] Corrosive sublimate (mercuric chloride) was used for whitening the skin and removing blemishes; camphor served as an unguent. These cosmetics in Fabia's basket remind us once again of her ancestor Celestina, one of whose six professions was the manufacture of cosmetics. Her stock was infinitely more varied, however, than Fabia's (see *Celestina*, Act I).

17. *There's ... peace*] R suggests that this passage means the deceived girl has asked Fabia for a love potion, presumably to bring her seducer back to her; such an interpretation is possible, but it is more likely that we have here a delicate reference to Fabia's act of restoring lost virginity, which was another of Celestina's six professions.

18. *flames of passion*] translates *fuego accidental*; the precise meaning of the adjective here is impossible to determine; it might, as well as the translation chosen, mean "sudden" or "contingent" (in the sense that a love produced by diabolic intervention would not be an essential or natural part of Ines's soul).

19. *All things ... lives*] See textual note. It is clear that the original text is elliptical and twisted in its syntax; the intention is reasonably clear—i.e., love both creates and destroys life—but the words do not fully encompass it.

20. *nature ... it*] See note 2.

21. *sextons ... back*] translation follows the interpretation of Ramón Rozzell in "Facistol," *Modern Language Notes* 66 (1951): 155-160, which explains that the sexton beat time for the singers on the choir desk; Fabia's back has been as brutally treated.

22. *Words ... stones*] translates *hay palos dentro, pues en mondadientes caben*, which means literally "there are blows (*palos*) inside, since they're contained even in toothpicks (*mondadientes*)." The humor depends on an untranslatable pun: a synonym for *mondadientes* is *palillos* ("little *palos*" or "little blows").

23. *dress ... window*] translates *para la reja de Inés/ importa bizarría*. During the daytime Spanish courtiers of Lope's day tended to wear dark, frequently black, clothing. When travelling, on festive occasions, and when going out at night to pay court to a lady, they usually wore more brightly colored and ornamented clothing. The color of the clothing worn by male actors thus may help to elucidate the time of the action and the situation. (See *Obras completas de Juan Ruiz de Alarcón*, ed. Agustín Millares Carlo, 1 [Mexico: Fondo de Cultura Económica, 1957]: 13, 826; also R. Dalmau and J. M.ª Soler Janer, *Historia del traje*, 1 [Barcelona: Dalmau y Jover, 1947]: 300.)

24. *I ... yesterday*] In the literature of the day there are numerous references to the witch's use of the teeth of hanged criminals for purposes of black magic. Celestina reports that a famous witch she had known had herself extracted seven teeth from a hanged man's mouth (*Celestina*, Act VII).

25. *dressed ... evening*] See note 23.

26. *dressed ... evening*] See note 23.

27. *extract ... house*] translates *sacar una dama de su casa*; a slight play on the word *sacar* ("take out") is involved; since to pull teeth out is *sacar dientes*, Tello manages to state the truth halfway and yet mislead his master.

28. *love ... hair*] See note 4.

29. *At ... King*] The king is Juan II of Castile (1406-1454); according to the *Crónica de Juan II* (Biblioteca de Autores Españoles, 68 [Madrid: Rivadeneyra, 1877]: 376), he married the Infanta Doña María de Aragón in 1418 in Medina del Campo itself and not in Valladolid. It may be assumed that the mention of this wedding fixes the time of the action of the play as after 1418, but see below, note 61. It is possible we should read the Spanish lines to mean that the King, while holding court in Valladolid at some later time, honored Alonso for his feats at the Medina wedding. Alonso should not, however, have been so much a stranger in Medina and to Inés if he had already appeared at a tournament in her own town. In vss. 1601-1602 below, Lope once again appears confused about the precise location of another royal wedding.

30. *games*] translates Spanish *sortija*, a sport in which the mounted knight rides at full tilt across a field and attempts to catch on the tip of his lance a ring (*sortija*) hanging above him.

31. *May ... end!*] The handsome young hunter Adonis, beloved of Aphrodite, was killed by a wild boar, his death actually serving to avenge Artemis against Aphrodite for the latter's having slain her devotee Hippolytus. Each year in spring and summer Adonis was allowed to return to earth; this annual death and resurrection symbolized the annual renewal of vegetation. So it is that Alonso very early in the play is linked with a classical symbol of manly beauty, tragic death, and resurrection.

32. *two ... suit*] See textual note. If *haréis* is substituted for *harán*, then the lines mean "The two of you [i.e., Inés and Alonso] will render his suit null and void."

33. *tertian ... salamander*] an involved passage developing the conceit of Alonso's love as a kind of malarial fever. Tertian fever (*tercianas*, vs. 902) completes its cycle of chills, fever, and sweating in forty-eight hours and begins again on the third day; the quartan fever (*cuartana*, vs. 910) cycle runs seventy-two hours, beginning again on the fourth day with chills. Because Alonso comes to see Inés in a feverish state every third day, Tello suggests he is suffering from a "tertian fever of love." Alonso seems to protest that the analogy is not apt, since his love never cools off, but later he takes up the comparison by admitting that on the fourth day, after seeing Inés, his fever is somewhat abated, as might be expected in an attack of quartan fever. If he were with her always, he adds, the fire of love would be so intense that only a salamander could endure it.

34. *Harlequin . . . gallows*] R says that Harlequin was accustomed to stand on a ladder propped against the supports of a tightrope and make fun of the acrobat performing on the rope. But it is, in fact, impossible now to ascertain what comic routine Lope had in mind. He alludes to it so casually that we must assume the contemporary audience was as familiar with it as we are with Charlie Chaplin's costume. The context of the remark actually suggests he is recalling a scene in which a frightened and trembling Harlequin tries to support a ladder. Such a scene is contained in the scenario of *The Fake Magician*, a *commedia dell'arte* piece done by the company of Flaminio Scala and published in Venice in 1611 (see *Scenarios of the "Commedia dell'Arte"* . . . trans. Henry F. Salerno [New York: New York University Press, 1967]). This play may have been performed in Spain; certainly Lope might have read the text; but it is equally likely that he is referring to some long-lost scenario. At the end of the sixteenth century, several companies of the Italian *commedia dell' arte* performed with great success in Spain, including that of Alberto Naselli (alias Zan Ganassa), who played there from 1574 to 1584 and is believed to have invented the character of Harlequin. Contemporary records also show that in 1587 Lope attended frequently the performances of the company of Tristano Martinelli, one of the most celebrated of Harlequins (see John V. Falconieri, "Historia de la *Commedia dell'Arte* en España," *Revista de Literatura* 11 [1957]: 3-37; 12 [1957]: 69-90).

35. *Holy . . . faint*] R notes that he calls on Saint Paul, remembering the latter's celebrated fall on the road to Damascus.

36. *wet clear through*] The *gracioso's* cowardice and fear, like those of Harlequin before him, frequently cause him to lose control of bladder or bowels and soil his clothing.

37. *"Inés . . . anyway"*] translates *Un poco te quiero, Inés*, which is the first line of a very popular folksong, of which the second line, *Yo te lo diré después* ("I'll tell you I love you some day"), is spoken by Tello later in vs. 1011. (See R, pp. 111-112, for documentation.)

38. *Who . . . liar*] See textual note. The brief joking exchange between the servants here openly identifies Alonso and Inés for the first time in the play with Calisto and Melibea because of the poetic ardor of their passion and their secret meetings by night. Tello, however, in the version suggested of vs. 1006, rejects being identified with Sempronio, the untrustworthy and cowardly servant of the original Calisto.

39. *I'll . . . day*] See note 37.

40. *Dearest . . . to him*] See textual note. When Rodrigo last appeared at Inés's house and formally asked for her hand, he came in the early morning (see vss. 733-734); Inés now speaks of an afternoon encounter with Rodrigo about which the audience has not been informed. The two or more lines missing from the text here possibly resolved the present difficulty; but it is equally possible that a few brief scenes have been omitted from the printed text of the play.

41. *at . . . breaks*] allusion to the horses which draw the sun's chariot through the heavens during the daylight hours.

42. *I . . . time*] allusion to the well-known dangerous attraction exerted by light on moths and butterflies and to the myth of the phoenix's self-immolation in a bonfire from the ashes of which arises a new phoenix.

43. *Listen . . . lines*] The five-line stanza here is called in Spanish *estribo* (vs. 1098), or "refrain." Alonso has, it is said, composed the refrain, and Tello has produced the *glosa* (vs. 1098) on it; a *glosa* is the elaborate form illustrated here in the following five stanzas, in which each stanza must end with the corresponding line of the original refrain. (The Spanish of vs. 1107 is puzzling, since *la* can refer only to the *glosa*, not to the *estribo*, and Inés appears to be asking whether the long *glosa* was composed by Alonso, even though the opposite has just been stated and though in vss. 1161-1163 she understands the long composition to be Tello's work.) The *estribo* is not original with Lope; R notes four previous occurrences of it in printed and manuscript texts (p. 116, n. 21).

44. *yesterday*] once again, a puzzling time reference. Inés appears to be alluding to a conversation with her father about marriage, but this "yesterday" cannot be understood as the day Rodrigo first appeared to ask for her hand, a scene witnessed in Act I, because a number of meetings between Alonso and Inés have taken place since then, and they had never even spoken directly to each other on the day Rodrigo first officially asked for her hand. The time scheme is either purposely imprecise, or this text of the play omits a scene in which Inés is officially informed by her father of Rodrigo's suit (see also note 40).

45. *already . . . husband*] an example of the device of "deceiving with the truth" (*engañar con la verdad*), much favored by Lope and his disciples. It is a form of dramatic irony achieved by using words in double meanings. Inés truly has a "husband," in the sense that she has promised to marry Alonso; but in the context her father understands that she has chosen Christ as her bridegroom.

46. *Feast . . . Cross*] in Spanish (vs. 1303), *la Cruz de Mayo*; this feast falls on May 3.

47. *King . . . Luna*] King Juan II came to the throne of Castile in 1406 as an infant; during his minority the kingdom was governed by a regent, his uncle the Infante Fernando de Antequera, who became King of Aragon in 1412. When Juan reached his majority at the age of fourteen, the weak young king quickly placed the powers of government largely in the hands of his great favourite, the brilliant Alvaro de Luna, who was made Lord High Constable of Castile in 1423. In 1453 Alvaro, who had suddenly fallen from favor, was beheaded by his royal master.

48. *And why . . . to it?*] translates *¿a qué efeto/es cédula de noche en una esquina?* (vss. 1365-1366). *Cédulas* ("papers," "documents," "posters") were frequently affixed to the walls of houses and buildings to publicize edicts or offer goods for sale.

49. *I think . . . yourself*] translates vss. 1379-1380; Lope plays with several bullfighting terms: *dejar la capa al toro* means to sacrifice something in order to avoid a greater danger, while *echar uno la capa al toro* is to distract the bull with the cape so that the bullfighter may escape danger.

50. *marry . . . impulses*] Here and throughout this scene the principal comic device is *double entendre* or *engañar con la verdad*. See note 45.

51. *Domine . . . festina*] See textual note. The English translation, in the King James version, is "Make haste to help me, O Lord" (Psalm 70:1).

52. *poor university student*] translates *gorrón*, literally a large cap (*gorra*). Because poor university students, who frequently lived by sponging and fraud, had the custom of wearing a short cape and cap which distinguished them from serious or richer students who wore mantles and a more clerical type of headgear, *gorrón* (more usually *capigorrón* or *capigorrista*) came also to designate not only an article of clothing but also this type of person. Since such students, if they became priests, usually, like Tello, took only minor orders, *gorrón*, *capigorrón*, *capigorrista* also designate such clerics (see C, DA, and note 68, below).

53. *Calahorra . . . Peláez*] In a late version of the epic *Poem of the Cid* given in the *Crónica de 1344* the name of Martín Peláez is borne by an originally cowardly character who later became one of the most valiant of the Cid's soldiers (see R. Menéndez Pidal, *Cantar de Mio Cid*, 1 [Madrid, 1908] : 131). This name, plus his pretended origin, Calahorra—a town located in the north of Spain and mentioned in C as famous for its heroism in Roman times—prompts Don Pedro's following remark.

54. *In . . . there*] The town of La Coruña, in Galicia, has never had a university.

55. *Have . . . ago*] In Spanish, Tello's answer (*Sí, señor, de vísperas*) to Don Pedro's inquiry about his ordination has an untranslatable double meaning. Don Pedro understands only that the student has taken minor orders which, probably, allow him to read the vesper service; but *de vísperas* also suggests "just last night," which, as the audience would appreciate, was when Tello decided to take on his clerical disguise. R and other editors prefer to think that *de vísperas* means the same thing as the set phrase *en vísperas de* ("on the eve of"), but Tello clearly announces that he is already ordained.

56. *In . . . conceived*] "Jousting" translates *las cañas*, a chivalric sport in which groups of knights fought each other with wooden poles, defending themselves with a leather buckler (*adarga*) which they were accustomed to decorate with devices, mottoes, or inscriptions cryptically alluding to their ladies. Tello has aided Alonso in concocting these devices.

57. *I . . . postage*] It was the custom for the person who received a letter to pay the postage costs.

58. *iugatoribus paternus*] The Latin is, as R remarks, either corrupted in this text or purposely without meaning. Fabia seems to mean Inés can attend the games because she has her father's permission; *paternus* obviously means "paternal," and *iugatoribus* may be meant to suggest "matrimonial" (*iugales*) or "game" (*iocus*).

59. *Should . . . now?*] The Spanish *¿Han de entrar?* (vs. 1557) has no expressed subject, nor can one be supplied from the context. It is reasonable to suppose, however, that the Constable might be referring to messengers, pages, petitioners, etc., waiting to see the King.

60. *Alcántara*] Alcántara, Santiago, and Calatrava, all founded in the twelfth century, are the major Spanish military orders, semi-religious in their orientation and dedicated to leading the fight against the Moors in defense of the Christian faith. Gentle birth was a prerequisite for membership, and for several centuries after their foundation, these organizations of noble knights were a major force in the life and government of the country.

61. *I . . . it*] The petition to the Pope was actually made in 1411 and not by the King, only a child of six then, but by the regent, his uncle Fernando. In these years the Church was rent by the Great Schism, so that the identity of the pope in question here is not clear: Gregory XII was the Roman pope at the time, but John XXIII had since 1410 been the schismatic pope, and Benedict XIII (the Aragonese Pedro de Luna), elected Pope of Avignon in 1394, continued to act as pope until his death in 1423, even though he had been officially replaced by John XXIII. The regent Fernando supported Pedro de Luna's claims to the papacy for many years. The *Crónica de la Orden de Alcántara* (cited in M, p. 114) gives the impression that Benedict XIII was indeed the pontiff involved. (See also *Crónica de Juan II*, ed. cit., pp. 338, 340, 360-361.) The chronological vagueness and inaccuracy of the play's historical background become apparent here, since previously there has been mention of the King's wedding in 1418 (see note 29), and Alvaro de Luna was not made Lord High Constable until 1423 (see note 47).

62. *I owe . . . side*] Since, as the previous note indicates, this scene deals with events of the year 1411, the Infante alluded to must be the regent Fernando; in 1412, after much maneuvering, he was chosen King of Aragon. It may be assumed that the Pope (Pedro de Luna?) was supporting Fernando's claim to the Aragonese throne. Fernando died in 1416 before his nephew Juan even reached his majority.

63. *first details . . . blood*] Vicente Ferrer, a Dominican friar from Valencia, began his fiery preaching in Castile against Jews and Moors in 1411 and begged the King, his mother Queen Catherine of Lancaster, and the Infante Fernando to segregate the Moors and Jews from the Christians in all the towns and cities of the kingdom, because the constant intermingling of the three religions might damage the faith of the Christians, especially those who had recently been converted from Islam or Judaism. In 1412, Queen Catherine (not the child King) ordered that Jews should wear tabards with a red mark on them and that green cowls stamped with a white crescent would be the obligatory dress of the Moors (*Crónica de Juan II*, ed. cit., p. 340).

64. *habit*] a habit of one of the chivalric orders (see note 60). Because of the preceding discussion of Alcántara, it is possible we should understand that Alonso was to wear its new habit with the green cross; but the original Knight of Olmedo, Juan de Vivero, was a Knight of Santiago (see Introduction, p. xv), as was Alvaro de Luna.

65. *city . . . wedding*] King Juan had two sisters, María and Catalina, neither of whom was married in Valladolid, where this scene appears to take place. María was married to Prince Alonso of Aragon in 1415; Catalina married the Infante Enrique of Aragon in Talavera in 1420 (*Crónica de Juan II*, ed. cit., pp. 362, 388).

66. *Indies*] not, of course, discovered at the time of the action, which leads R to believe these lines were written before the play for other purposes; but anachronisms of this type are not infrequent in Lope (see note 81).

67. *Oh harsh . . . divided*] This whole monologue, a *romancillo* in Spanish, also appears, with many variants, in Act III of Lope's *Dorotea* (1632). Vs. 1657 of the Spanish contains an untranslatable play on words, since *partir* means both "to leave" and "to divide."

68. *students . . . wear*] See note 52. Poor students particularly wore Vandyke collars (see note 5) without the starch and fine lace felt to be essential by fashionable gentlemen. As R points out (p. 139), Don Quijote wore a collar of this inferior type (II:18).

69. *stars . . . together*] See notes 2 and 14.

70. *dreams*] *sueños* in Spanish (vs. 1746); H, noting that Alonso never recounts his dreams, suggests some lines may be missing here. However, it is likely that Tello's scoffing discourages Alonso from relating the dream; instead, he describes a scene he has witnessed that seems to confirm the warnings of his dreams. B offers another possible solution (not followed here), namely, that *sueños* is here used in the unusual sense of "presentiments."

71. *windows*] Distinguished spectators like Don Pedro and his family usually saw bullfights, tournaments, and plays from the windows or balcony of the houses surrounding the square where the performance took place.

72. *Bad thrusts*] translates *malas suertes*; a *suerte* in bullfighting is each one of the crucial moments or movements in the bullfight and cannot be precisely rendered in English. See also, e.g., vss. 1821, 1840, 1860 of the Spanish. These noblemen are not fighting on foot with cape and sword but mounted on horseback and armed with a lance (*rejón*) with a notch near the tip; the bullfighter seeks to wound the bull by inserting his lance into the animal so that it breaks off at the notch.

73. *lance*] See previous note.

74. *Exit Tello*] See textual note to vs. 1931.

75. *bulls*] translates *algún mozo de San Lucas* (vs. 1995); the bull is the traditional symbol of Saint Luke the Evangelist. The banter about the bull's tearing Tello's pants off, thus exposing him to ridicule for indecent exposure, continues to the end of this scene and is probably based, as noted in M (pp. 121-124), on the burlesque ballad of Don Bueso, a foolish old man who rips his trousers on mounting his horse; later, while courting a pretty young girl, he falls off the horse and thus displays to the laughing spectators—and the sun—his naked posterior.

76. *Nero . . . Tarpeia*] translates vss. 2051-2053 of the Spanish, which recall the opening lines of a famous old ballad: "Mira Nero de Tarpeya/ a Roma cómo se ardía" ("From Tarpeia, Nero watches how Rome burns"). It has been alleged that Nero set the fire himself and watched the city burn either from the stage of his private theater or from the Capitoline Hill, where the Tarpeian Rock is located.

77. *red . . . pleasure*] translates *y que por los labios rojos/ pagaba en perlas el gusto* (vss. 2059-2060), which literally says that "through her red lips she

paid in pearls for the pleasure," or, in other words, that the pearls of her teeth were revealed as her lips parted in a smile of pleasure.

78. *Infante*] presumably Fernando de Antequera; see note 47.

79. *dressed . . . evening*] See note 23.

80. *I'm sorry . . . see you*] In Spanish this speech (vss. 2176-2225) is developed as a *glosa* (see note 43) on an old, anonymous, and very well-known stanza, utilized by many other writers (most notably Cervantes in his valedictory dedication [1616] to *Persiles y Sigismunda*), which runs as follows:

> Puesto ya el pie en el estribo,
> con las ansias de la muerte,
> señora, aquesto te escribo,
> pues partir no puedo vivo
> cuanto más volver a verte.

> (One foot already in the stirrup,
> possessed by the fear of death,
> I write you this, my lady,
> for I cannot hope to leave alive
> and even less to see you more.)

The word *ansias* (vs. 2) means both "longing" and "anguish," "affliction," or "torment"; it is clear that by this point Alonso experiences both of these emotions with regard to death.

81. *harquebus*] an anachronism; the shoulder gun did not come into practical use until the mid-fifteenth century and even then on a very limited scale because of its rude and unwieldy construction. Yet the use of such a weapon here is poetically, if not historically, appropriate; since gunpowder and firearms signalled the end of medieval chivalry, the murder of this mirror of knighthood by such nonchivalric means acquires a certain symbolic significance.

82. *money*] Alonso assumes that the men are highway robbers.

83. *Infante*] presumably his uncle, the Infante Fernando de Antequera (see note 47).

84. *cross of Alcántara*] See note 64.

85. *despite . . . rivals*] The long reign of Juan II was almost constantly agitated by uprisings of nobles against him, especially by the machinations of his cousins, the Infantes of Aragon.

86. *Inés*] See textual note to vss. 2709-2710.

APPENDIX: SYNOPSIS OF VERSIFICATION

Since an English prose translation cannot convey the fluidity and variety of Lope's versification, the following analysis of meters used has been provided to suggest at least the variety at his command. For a definition of these meters, see S. Griswold Morley and Courtney Bruerton, *The Chronology of Lope de Vega's "Comedias"* (New York: MLA, 1940), pp. 11-13. Only lines of verse have been counted; the prose letter in Act II does not enter into the line count, nor do the three lines of verse presumably missing from this text of the play (at least two after vs. 1017 and at least one after vs. 2709).

ACT I

Lines	Verse Form	Total Lines in Passage
1-30	décimas	30
31-74	redondillas	44
75-182	romance (í-a)	108
183-406	redondillas	224
407-460	romance (a-a)	54
461-490	décimas	30
491-502	redondillas	12
503-516	soneto	14
517-532	redondillas	16
533-570	romance (a-e)	38
571-622	redondillas	52
623-706	romance (a-a)	84
707-786	redondillas	80
787-885	romance (e-o)	99
886-887	seguidilla (media)	2

ACT II

888-1033	redondillas	146
1034-1093	décimas	60
1094-1101	redondillas	8
1102-1106	quintilla (6-syllable)	5
1107-1110	redondilla	4
1111-1160	quintillas (coplas reales)	50
1161-1248	redondillas	88

1249-1330	romance (e–a)	82
1331-1391	tercetos	61
1392-1463	redondillas	72
1464-1551	romance (e–o)	88
1552-1607	redondillas	56
1608-1657	romancillo (í–a)	50
1658-1725	redondillas	68
1726-1811	romance (a–a)	86

ACT III

1812-2011	redondillas	200
2012-2075	romance (o–o)	64
2076-2175	redondillas	100
2176-2225	quintillas (coplas reales)	50
2226-2249	redondillas	24
2250-2301	romance (í–e)	52
2302-2341	octavas reales	40
2342-2371	décimas	30
2372-2375	seguidilla	4
2376-2383	redondillas	8
2384-2390	seguidilla	7
2391-2414	redondillas	24
2415-2506	romance (e–o)	92
2507-2586	redondillas	80
2587-2729	romance (e–o)	143

Summary Figures for the Whole Play

Verse Forms	Total Lines (No.)	Total Lines (%)
redondillas	1306	47.8
romance	990	36.3
décimas	150	5.5
quintillas	100	3.9
tercetos	61	2.2
romancillo	50	1.8
octavas reales	40	1.5
soneto	14	0.5
seguidillas	13	0.5
Totals	2729	100.0